# Woman's Day
## PLAIN & FANCY
## GROUND BEEF
## COOKBOOK

# Edited by Jeri Laber

# Woman's Day
## PLAIN & FANCY
## GROUND BEEF
## COOKBOOK

 Random House · New York

All rights reserved under International and Pan-American Copyright
Conventions. Published in the United States by Random House,
Inc., New York, and simultaneously in Canada by Random House of
Canada Limited, Toronto.

Library of Congress Cataloging in Publication Data
Main entry under title:
Women's day plain and fancy ground beef cookbook.
Includes index.
1. Cookery (Beef)    I. Laber, Jeri.    II. Woman's day.
III. Title: Plain and fancy ground beef.
TX749.W64        641.6'6'2        78-57135
ISBN 0-394-41372-5

Manufactured in the United States of America

2 3 4 5 6 7 8 9

First Edition

ILLUSTRATIONS BY LILLY LANGOTSKY

# CONTENTS

# INTRODUCTION
## by Jeri Laber

AMERICA IS A NATION of hamburger-lovers—who can deny it? The average American, according to recent statistics, consumes almost forty pounds of ground beef a year, a figure that keeps increasing. And for good reason, too: Ground beef is not only economical and nutritious, but as versatile as any food can be. Children love hamburgers; so do folks on the go. Though basic to barbecues and casual dining, ground meat, as this book will show, is equally at home at the most elegant dinner parties.

Hamburgers are not an American invention. Meat has been ground or shredded for eating throughout history, going back to the times of the ancient Egyptians. Indeed, it was only about a hundred years ago that ground beef was introduced to our shores, brought over by immigrants from Hamburg, Germany (hence the name). The first mention in print of a "hamburg steak" was in the Boston *Journal* in 1884. The first broiled hamburgers served on toasted buns are said to have been introduced in St. Louis at the Louisiana Purchase Exposition of 1904. They were obviously an immediate hit.

Popular as they are, even hamburgers can get boring when they're served too frequently. "What? Not hamburgers again!" is, unfortunately, a common outcry in those homes where the same old basic hamburgers are served over and over again. That's the reason for this book: it will show you hundreds of different ways to make ground meat continually interesting, varied and delicious.

A perfect hamburger or ground-beef dish requires more than a good recipe, however: it is important to use good, fresh meat. The best possible meat is not always the most expensive. Indeed, sirloin, filet mignon and other expensive cuts of meat are usually too lean for hamburgers and many other ground-beef dishes. A hamburger needs some fat in order to hold its shape and be juicy and tender.

We prefer hamburger meat that contains between 10 and 15 percent fat, considerably less than the 30 percent allowed under government regulations. Unless you grind your own meat or your butcher is willing to analyze the fat content for you—and there are few who will—you must rely on what you see in making a selection. Study ground beef before buying it and you'll soon learn to tell when it is too fatty. It should be a healthy, rich red color with fairly frequent flecks of white fat. Compare the different packages at your supermarket, just as you do when selecting a package of bacon.

Though all beef is inspected for wholesomeness, not all markets label the packages of meat they sell with information about content. "Prime" cuts, the most tender, fine-textured meats, are very expensive and not generally available in supermarkets. The grades you are most likely to find at your local supermarket are "Choice," "Good" and "Standard." "Choice," the most popular grade in this country, contains less fat in its marbling than "Prime" and is not quite as tender or flavorful, but it is still excellent in quality. "Good" is often branded "economy meat" in local stores. "Standard" tends to be too bland and tough for our liking.

Ground chuck, or beef labeled "lean," is, in general, the best meat to use in most of the recipes in this book. Ground round, or "very lean," is more expensive, and should be saved for meat loaf or for times when you wish to cut down on fat in your diet. Some supermarket meat packages are simply labeled "ground beef"; thus labeled, they can legally contain meat from any edible part of the animal. Ground-meat packages labeled "hamburger" may also contain inferior cuts, as well as added beef fat and/or seasoning.

"Meat-loaf mixture," a combination of ground beef, veal and pork, may be used as a substitute for ground beef when making meat loaf and other dishes.

Some stores sell ground beef that has been extended with textured vegetable protein (usually soy). Soy protein is also sold separately, and you can add it yourself if you wish to extend your meat. Extended ground beef usually has a ratio of about 75 percent to 25 percent extender. A pound of ground beef and a packet of extender will yield 1½ pounds of extended beef.

You can also use other extenders: to 1 pound of ground meat, add ½ cup of soft bread soaked in an equal amount of seasoned milk or stock, or add 1 cup of processed cereal such as oatmeal or corn flakes to each pound of ground beef. Other heathful additions might include ½ cup grated raw carrots or potatoes, or ¼ to ½ cup of bran or wheat germ.

Mix all extenders as lightly as possible with the meat, using a fork or your hands. If you use an extender that has been seasoned, adjust the seasoning of the beef accordingly. Since extended beef tends to be considerably softer than unextended beef, do not use it in recipes for stews or sauces requiring long simmering, or the meat might fall apart.

If you are stretching meat in order to save money, be sure to compare costs. Some people end up using products which are more expensive per pound than the meat itself.

If you are adding extenders to make your burgers more nutritious, bear in mind that ground beef is extremely nutritious to begin with, full of good protein. Beef contains all the necessary amino acids which the body needs for growing, to repair tissues, to regenerate blood and help build resistance to infection. It is also an abundant source of B-complex vitamins, as well as essential minerals, iron, copper and phosphorus. So if your child craves hamburgers, don't worry: it's healthy, body-building food.

Full of protein and energy, ground beef is excellent food for diet watchers. A broiled lean ¼-pound burger contains less than 200 calories.

Ground beef is perishable. Raw hamburger should be wrapped lightly and stored in the coldest part of the refrigerator; its refrigerator-shelf life is one to two days. Cooked and covered, ground meat will keep in the refrigerator for three to four days. Gravy and meat broth, also quite perishable, should be cooled quickly and then refrigerated immediately; keep gravy only for a day or two, unless you heat it up to a boil frequently.

To freeze ground beef, package it in moisture- and vapor-proof wrappings, such as freezer bags, polyethylene film or bags, or heavy-weight aluminum foil. Wrap the meat tight, pressing out as much air as possible, and seal the packages well with freezer or masking tape. Always label the package, noting the quantity and kind of meat contained and the date that it was frozen. Ground meat will keep in the freezer for three to four months if stored at 0° F. or below.

Don't freeze ground beef in very large quantities. It may not freeze rapidly enough if you do and, what's more, you will be forced to thaw it all out before using it, which may prove wasteful. Instead, freeze ground meat in 1- or 1½-pound packages, or divide the beef into patties and wrap and freeze them individually. When you freeze meat in patties, you can remove as many as you like at a given time without worrying about waste.

Specific tips on cooking and freezing various kinds of ground-beef dishes are included in the introductions to each of the chapters in this book. But there are certain general rules which apply to all ground-beef preparations. First and foremost, always handle ground meat lightly, no matter how you are cooking it. Overhandled meat becomes dense, tough and rubbery. It is also important, whenever possible, to use fresh ingredients in these dishes. Fresh vegetables and herbs are not costly. Preparation time may be slightly greater, but the difference in taste is truly remarkable!

There are over 250 recipes for ground beef in this cookbook. Some are easy as can be; others are a little more complex. Each will show you another delicious way to cook that perennial favorite—ground beef. Use these recipes and you will find that hamburgers and ground-beef dishes can be a special treat every time you serve them.

# SOUPS

❀❀❀❀❀❀❀❀❀❀❀❀❀❀❀❀❀❀❀❀❀❀❀❀❀❀

MOST OF THE SOUPS offered here are hearty enough to serve as a main course. A loaf of hot, buttered French bread and a fresh green salad are all you need to add. You can also serve the soups as openers to a full meal, of course, or try that old-time favorite—soup and sandwich.

Soups will keep in the refrigerator for a couple of days, and they can also be frozen. Freeze them in plastic containers or freezer jars, leaving a one-inch space at the top to allow for expansion during freezing. Label each container with the name of the soup, the number of servings and when it was prepared. Most soups will keep well for six or more months in your freezer.

Even if a soup recipe calls for potatoes, keep them out of the soup if you plan to freeze it. Potatoes become mushy and do not freeze well; add them to frozen soups when you are reheating the soups for serving. Remind yourself to add the potatoes by marking this information on the package label.

To reheat frozen soup, place the container in a pot of barely simmering water until the soup is loose enough to transfer to a saucepan. Then simply heat the soup and serve.

# Beef-Rice Consommé

1 pound ground beef
2 onions, minced
2 tablespoons butter
1 cup uncooked rice
4 cups beef broth
1 pimiento, chopped
Few sprigs of parsley, chopped
2 drops hot pepper sauce

Cook the beef, breaking it up with a fork, until browned and done; drain off fat and set the beef aside. Cook the onion in the butter until golden. Add the rice and brown lightly. Stir in 2 cups of the broth. Bring to a boil, cover and cook for about 30 minutes, or until the rice is tender. Add the cooked beef, the rest of the broth and the remaining ingredients during the last 5 minutes of cooking. Makes 4–6 servings.

# Kreplach Soup

*A great Jewish favorite is chicken soup with kreplach—dumplings that can be filled with a variety of fillings.*

1 tablespoon oil
½ pound ground beef
½ cup minced onion
½ teaspoon salt
Pepper
2 eggs
1 tablespoon water
½ teaspoon salt
2 cups flour
4 cups strong chicken broth

Heat the oil in a skillet; add the meat and onions and cook for 10 minutes, stirring frequently. Drain off excess fat. Add the salt and pepper and set aside. Work the eggs, water and salt into the flour and knead until the dough is smooth and elastic. Roll out as thin as possible, and cut into 3-inch squares. Cover with a damp towel so that the dough doesn't dry out. Place a tablespoon of the meat mixture on each square. Fold over to make a triangle and press the edges together, moistening them with a little water. Drop the kreplach into a gallon of boiling salted water and cook for about 20 minutes, or until they rise to the top. Drain well. Add to the hot chicken broth. Makes 4 servings.

# Hamburger-Tomato Soup with Rice Dumplings

1 pound ground beef
1½ tablespoons butter
1 can (28 ounces) tomatoes, undrained
1 envelope onion soup mix
¼ teaspoon paprika
1 can (16 ounces) red kidney beans, undrained
1½ cups water
1 teaspoon salt
¼ teaspoon pepper
1 bay leaf
Rice Dumplings (see below)

In a Dutch oven or a 12-inch skillet with a cover, brown the beef in butter, stirring with a fork to break up the meat. Drain off excess fat. Add the remaining ingredients except the Rice Dumplings. Bring to a boil, cover and simmer for 10 minutes. Remove bay leaf. Drop dumpling batter by tablespoonfuls into the soup. Cover and simmer for 20 minutes without removing the cover. Makes 6 servings.

RICE DUMPLINGS

1¾ cups flour
2 teaspoons baking powder
½ teaspoon salt
3 tablespoons shortening
¾ cup cooked rice, cold
2 tablespoons minced parsley
½ cup milk
1 egg

Sift the flour, baking powder and salt. Cut in the shortening. Add the rice and parsley. In a separate bowl beat the milk and egg together with a fork. Add to the flour mixture, stirring with a fork until the dry ingredients are dampened. (Mixture will be stiff, but do not add more milk.)

## Meatball Soup

*A hearty main dish soup with a raw egg added at the last moment, Chinese-style.*

1 pound ground beef
1 large clove garlic, minced
1 tablespoon chopped parsley
½ teaspoon marjoram
½ teaspoon basil
1 teaspoon salt
¼ teaspoon pepper
2 eggs
Flour
5 cups water
1 cup canned tomatoes, undrained
3 beef bouillon cubes
2 small bay leaves, crumbled
3 tablespoons uncooked rice

Mix the beef, garlic, parsley, marjoram and basil with ½ teaspoon of the salt, the pepper and 1 of the eggs. Form the mixture into tiny balls; dredge with flour. In a large pot, bring the water, tomatoes, bouillon cubes, the remaining ½ teaspoon salt and the bay leaves to a boil. Add the meatballs and rice. Cover the pot and simmer for 50–60 minutes. Beat the remaining egg slightly and, just before serving, stir it into the soup. Makes 4–5 servings.

## Chunky Meatball Soup

5 cups beef broth
1 pound ground beef
1 egg
½ teaspoon salt
½ teaspoon pepper
12 scallions (green onion), sliced
1 cup thinly sliced celery
1 cup thinly sliced carrots
½ small head cabbage, shredded
2 medium potatoes, peeled, in chunks
2 tomatoes, peeled, in eighths
½ cup uncooked rice
2 bay leaves
1 teaspoon basil
3 tablespoons soy sauce

Simmer the broth in a large pot. Mix the beef, egg, salt and pepper and shape into 1½-inch balls. Drop into the broth. Add the scallions, celery, carrots, cabbage, potatoes, tomatoes, rice, bay leaves and basil. Cover and simmer for about 30 minutes, stirring occasionally. Remove the bay leaves and stir in the soy sauce. Makes 6 servings.

# Mexican Meatball Soup

*Spicy and lively, a popular Mexican soup.*

½ pound ground beef
½ pound ground pork
1 egg
1 tablespoon chopped mint or 1 teaspoon oregano
¼ cup soft bread crumbs
¼ teaspoon pepper
Salt
2 quarts beef broth
1 cup tomato purée
½ cup chopped onion
1 clove garlic, crushed
2 teaspoons chili powder

Thoroughly mix the beef, pork, egg, mint or oregano, bread crumbs, pepper and 1 teaspoon salt. Form into balls the size of filberts. Combine the remaining ingredients and bring to a boil. Add the meatballs, cover and simmer for about 45 minutes. Add salt to taste. Makes 6 servings.

## Cabbage-Meatball Soup

A *wonderful use for leftover Tomato Sauce (see recipe p. 263).*

2 cans (10½ ounces each) beef broth
3 soup cans water
8 cups finely shredded cabbage
4 cups Tomato Sauce (p. 263)
Pinch of sugar (optional)

In a large saucepan bring the broth and water to a boil. Add the cabbage, bring again to a boil and cook, uncovered, until the cabbage is tender, 12–15 minutes. Stir in the spaghetti and meatball sauce and add the sugar if you like. Heat well. Makes 6 servings.

## Vegetable Potpourri Soup

1¼ pounds ground beef
¼ cup fine dry bread crumbs
1 clove garlic, crushed
2 tablespoons minced onion
1 egg
2 teaspoons salt
½ teaspoon pepper
1 can (16 ounces) tomatoes, undrained
2 tablespoons butter
4 cans (10½ ounces each) condensed vegetable soup
Leftovers (peas, mushrooms, lettuce, etc.)

Mix the beef, bread crumbs, garlic, onion, egg, salt and pepper with ½ cup of the juice from the tomatoes. Mix well and shape into 1-inch balls. Brown on all sides in butter in a skillet or Dutch oven. Add the condensed vegetable soup, 1 soup can of water and the tomatoes, broken into pieces, along with the remaining juice. Mix lightly, taking care not to break the meatballs, and heat through. Add any good leftovers: a few peas, a few sliced mushrooms, some chopped wilted lettuce. Makes 6 servings.

## Rich Beef and Vegetable Soup

*Serve with a big pan of hot cornbread.*

1 pound ground beef
1 can (16 ounces) tomatoes, mashed, undrained
2 onions, chopped
3 large potatoes, peeled and chopped
½ teaspoon pepper
¼ teaspoon oregano
½ teaspoon garlic powder
Pinch of sweet basil
½ can (16 ounces) whole-kernel corn
½ pound cut green beans
½ cup uncooked rice
Salt

Break up the beef in a large pot. Add 1 quart water, tomatoes, onions and potatoes. Add the pepper and herbs and simmer slowly for 1 hour. Add the corn, green beans and rice and simmer for 30 minutes longer. Add salt to taste, about 3 teaspoons. Makes 7–8 servings.

## Dixie Vegetable Soup

Soupbone
2 pounds ground beef
1 chicken bouillon cube
1 beef bouillon cube
1 tablespoon salt
Pepper
2½ quarts water (or half water and half stock)
2 stalks celery, cut coarse
1 large onion, chopped
2 16-ounce cans tomatoes
1 package (10 ounces) frozen cut okra
2 packages (10 ounces each) frozen succotash
1 package (10 ounces) frozen butter beans
¼ cup uncooked macaroni
1 potato, peeled, in large chunks

In a large covered pot, cook the soupbone, beef, bouillon cubes, salt and pepper in 2½ quarts of water for 1 hour, breaking the beef apart with a spoon and letting the mixture boil gently. Add the remaining ingredients and simmer for 5–6 hours. This soup improves with reheating. Makes 6–8 servings.

# Vegetable-Beef Soup

½ pound ground beef
1 large onion, chopped
1 clove garlic, minced
½ cup chopped celery and leaves
3 carrots, chopped
½ cup diced green beans
2 potatoes, peeled and diced
1 tablespoon flour
1½ teaspoons salt
¼ teaspoon pepper
Dash of cayenne

Brown the meat in a large pot, stirring to break it up. Add the onion and garlic and cook until yellowed. Add the remaining vegetables and cook, stirring often, for 3 minutes. If there is much fat in the pot, remove all but about 1 tablespoon and save for other purposes. Stir in the flour; add 6 cups boiling water, the salt, pepper and cayenne. Cover and simmer for about 20 minutes, or until the vegetables are tender. Makes 4 servings.

# Lentil Soup with Ground Beef

*So rich and so thick it could be called a casserole. Serve with a dollop of sour cream on top and a leafy salad on the side.*

1½ cups lentils, rinsed and picked over
3 tablespoons butter
3 medium onions, chopped
1 clove garlic, minced
1½ pounds ground beef
2 beef bouillon cubes
2 tablespoons uncooked rice
½ teaspoon sugar
1 teaspoon cumin
½ teaspoon pepper
1 tablespoon cider vinegar
Salt

Bring 1 quart of water to a boil in a saucepan, add the lentils and cook for 20 minutes. Drain, reserving the liquid and the lentils separately. Heat the butter in a deep skillet and sauté the onions and garlic until tender, stirring occasionally. Stir in the beef and brown well, breaking it up with a fork. Drain off excess fat. Dissolve the bouillon cubes in 2⅓ cups of the reserved liquid and add to the meat mixture. Cover and simmer for about 10 minutes. Stir in the lentils, rice, sugar, cumin and pepper. Bring to a boil, reduce heat, cover and simmer for about 30 minutes, or until the lentils and rice are tender and much of the liquid has been absorbed. (If liquid absorbs too rapidly, add more.) Stir in the vinegar and add salt to taste. Makes 6 servings.

# MAIN DISHES
## and CASSEROLES

✧)✧)✧)✧)✧)✧)✧)✧)✧)✧)✧)✧)✧)✧)✧)✧)✧)✧)✧)✧)✧)✧)✧)✧)

❖❖❖❖❖❖❖❖❖❖❖❖❖❖❖❖❖❖❖❖❖❖❖❖❖❖❖❖❖❖

THE MAIN DISHES in this chapter vary from dinner-type hamburgers to delicate meat-filled crêpes. Hamburger patties,
when served for dinner, should usually be larger than their
lunchtime counterparts: Make three or even two patties
from each pound of ground beef (except in certain of the
following recipes where we suggest smaller patties, generally because there is a rich sauce).

There's no reason to avoid serving ground beef to guests.
It's not *what* you serve but how you serve it that counts,
and the fact is that a well-prepared hamburger or hamburger dish is far more delectable than an expensive
but mediocre steak.

Casseroles are also wonderful main dishes, and we
include lots of good casserole recipes here, perfect for
when you want to make a small quantity of ground beef
go a long way.

Most casseroles are also ideal for freezing, usually for
up to six months. The most practical way to freeze a
casserole is to line the casserole itself with aluminum foil
before adding the food. Bake, cool, then put the casserole
in the freezer. When the food is frozen, lift it with the foil
from the casserole and wrap it securely with additional

foil. Label the package with a description of the dish, noting how many servings it will provide and when it was baked. When you wish to reheat it, remove the wrapping and put the frozen block of food back into the original casserole for heating in a 325° to 350° F. oven. Most frozen casseroles will take at least 1½ times the original baking time to reheat completely.

Do not overcook casseroles if you plan to freeze them, for they will cook more while reheating. If the casserole contains a lot of oil or fat, skim off the fat after the casserole has chilled and then freeze the casserole.

Potatoes become mushy when frozen; leave them out of casserole dishes and add them later, while reheating. Make a note of this as a reminder on the freezer label.

Do not worry if a sauce has separated during freezing. Simply whip or stir the sauce while reheating.

# Hamburgers with Onions, Swedish Style

1½ pounds ground beef
3 tablespoons butter
2–4 yellow onions, sliced
1 green pepper, in rings
Salt and pepper
Parsley potatoes, pickled cucumbers (optional)

Shape the meat into 4 or 5 patties, handling it as little as possible. Melt half the butter in a skillet, add the onions and sauté over low heat until golden. Add the pepper rings and ½ cup boiling water. Season with salt and pepper to taste, remove from heat and keep warm. Season the meat on both sides and sauté it in the remaining butter in the skillet until it is of desired doneness. Top each patty with the onion mixture and serve with potatoes and cucumbers if desired. Makes 4–5 servings.

# Hamburger Cups with Mushrooms

*Savory Butter adds a very special touch.*

1½ pounds ground beef
12 large mushrooms
Salt and pepper
Savory Butter (see next page)

Shape the meat into 5 or 6 thick patties, making a large depression in the center of each. Place the patties in a shallow baking dish. Cut off the lower part of the mushroom stems and put the mushrooms around the meat. Bake in a preheated 400° F. oven for 10–20 minutes, depending on the degree of doneness desired. Turn the mushrooms once during cooking and sprinkle with salt and pepper to taste. Remove the meat to a platter, putting 2 mushrooms in the center of each patty. Top with a scant spoonful of Savory Butter. Makes 5–6 servings.

SAVORY BUTTER

⅓ cup butter
2 tablespoons chopped parsley
2 tablespoons chopped scallion (green onion) tops

Cream the butter; then add the parsley and scallions.

# Hamburgers in Caper Sauce

2 pounds ground beef
½ cup evaporated milk
1 egg, slightly beaten
1 teaspoon salt
¼ teaspoon pepper
½ teaspoon garlic powder
Caper Sauce (see next page)

Mix all ingredients together except the Caper Sauce. Shape the meat into 6 patties and panbroil in a skillet, turning once and cooking to desired doneness. Remove to a warm platter and pour sauce over meat. Makes 6 servings.

CAPER SAUCE

3 tablespoons butter
3 tablespoons sour cream
1 bottle (2¼ ounces) capers, drained

Melt the butter in the unwashed skillet used for cooking the meat patties. Add the sour cream and capers and heat through, scraping the pan and stirring well.

# Hamburgers with Creole Sauce

1 small onion, minced
1 small green pepper, minced
¼ cup sliced mushrooms
2 tablespoons butter
¼ cup tomato paste
1 can (16 ounces) tomatoes, undrained
½ teaspoon thyme
Salt and pepper
2 teaspoons lemon juice
2 pounds ground beef
Cayenne

Sauté the onion, green pepper and mushrooms in butter in a saucepan over low heat for 5 minutes. Add the tomato paste and tomatoes, bring to a boil and simmer, uncovered, for 10 minutes. Add the thyme, salt and pepper to taste and the lemon juice and set sauce aside. Shape the meat into 6 patties, handling them as little as possible. Season with salt and cayenne and broil to desired doneness. Serve with the sauce. Makes 6 servings.

## Ranchero Hamburgers and Fried Eggs

*After a long day outdoors, nothing tastes better than these hamburgers and eggs served with home fried potatoes, sourdough bread and plenty of cold beer.*

2 pounds ground beef
½ cup plus 2 tablespoons butter
1 tablespoon tarragon vinegar
2 tablespoons chopped chives
1½ tablespoons capers
6 eggs
Salt and pepper

Form the beef into 6 large patties. Melt ½ cup of the butter in a small saucepan over low heat. Remove all the milky curds that form on top. Add the vinegar, chives and capers and keep warm. Panbroil the patties to desired doneness. Using another skillet, panfry the eggs in the remaining 2 tablespoons butter, timing it so that the meat and eggs will be done at the same time. Season eggs and meat with salt and freshly ground pepper to taste. Top each patty with a fried egg and spoon seasoned butter over each serving. Makes 3–6 servings.

# Hamburgers with Creamy Dijon Sauce

2 pounds ground beef
1 egg
3 tablespoons minced onion
1 teaspoon salt
1 teaspoon pepper
¼ teaspoon thyme
Flour
1 tablespoon oil
1 tablespoon butter
2 tablespoons chopped shallots or scallions (green onion)
½ cup white vermouth
1 tablespoon Dijon mustard
½ cup heavy cream
Chopped parsley

Mix the meat, egg, onion, salt, pepper and thyme and form into 6 patties. Roll lightly in flour and sauté in oil and butter for several minutes on each side. Remove the patties to a warm plate. Sauté the shallots or scallions for a minute in the pan, add the vermouth and boil the liquid down until it is reduced by half. In a bowl mix the mustard with driblets of the heavy cream until entirely blended. Pour into the pan; boil until lightly thickened. Add the parsley and pour the sauce over the patties. Makes 6 servings.

# Sauerbraten Patties

3 slices stale bread
1 pound ground beef
1 medium onion, minced
1 egg
1½ teaspoons salt
2 tablespoons butter
½ cup vinegar
1½ cups water
10 cloves
5 bay leaves
8 gingersnaps, crumbled
½ pound wide noodles, cooked, hot

Soak the bread in a little warm water; crumble. Add the meat, onion, egg and salt; mix well. Shape into 4 patties. Brown on both sides in the butter. Add the vinegar, water, cloves, bay leaves and gingersnaps; cover, and simmer for about 1 hour. Remove bay leaves. Serve over hot cooked noodles. Makes 4 servings.

# Polish-Style Hamburgers

*They simmer in sour cream and are served with french-fried onions.*

1 onion, peeled
1 carrot, peeled
1 stalk celery
1 medium potato, peeled
Few sprigs of parsley
¾ pound ground beef
2 slices bread, crumbled
1 egg
1½ teaspoons seasoned salt
¼ teaspoon pepper
2 tablespoons butter
1 cup sour cream
French-fried onion rings

Force the onion, carrot, celery, potato and parsley through the medium blade of a food chopper or chop in a food processor. Combine with the meat, bread crumbs, egg, salt and pepper and mix lightly but thoroughly. Shape into 6 patties and brown quickly on both sides in butter. Remove the meat from the skillet and blend the sour cream into the drippings. Put the patties back in the skillet, cover and simmer for about 10–15 minutes. Top with onion rings. Makes 3 servings.

# Hamburgers with
# Mushroom-Almond Stuffing

¼ cup butter
¼ cup chopped mushrooms
¼ cup slivered almonds
¾ cup fine dry bread crumbs
¼ cup chopped parsley
½ teaspoon poultry seasoning
2 tablespoons lemon juice
¼ teaspoon each salt and pepper
2 pounds ground beef
Steak sauce (optional)

Melt the butter in a skillet and add the mushrooms and
almonds. Sauté, stirring, for a few minutes. Add the remaining ingredients except the beef, mix well, and set
aside. Divide the beef into 6 portions. Divide the filling
among the portions and shape the beef into balls, covering
the filling completely. Flatten slightly and cook as desired.
Season to taste or serve with your favorite steak sauce.
Makes 6 servings.

# Pesto Hamburger Steaks

*Pesto sauce, generally thought of as a spaghetti sauce, makes a scrumptious filling for hamburger steaks.*

1 cup fresh basil leaves
1 cup pine nuts or walnuts
2 cloves garlic, crushed
½ cup olive oil
½ cup freshly grated Parmesan cheese
3 pounds ground beef
Butter
Salt and pepper

Put the basil, nuts, garlic, oil and Parmesan cheese in a blender and spin until smooth. Spread half the meat evenly into a 16-by-8-inch rectangle and cut it into 4-inch squares, using a ruler. Repeat with the remaining portion of meat. Spread Pesto on half the squares, leaving a ½-inch margin around the edges. Place the remaining squares on top, and seal the edges by crimping them with your fingers. Place the patties on a lightly buttered broiling pan and broil them for 6–8 minutes, turning once. Just before serving, spread with a little butter and sprinkle with salt and pepper. Makes 8 servings.

# Hamburger with Béarnaise Sauce

*This classic French sauce is also heavenly on fish and eggs.*

½ cup white wine
2 tablespoons tarragon vinegar
2 tablespoons chopped shallots or scallions (green onion)
2 crushed peppercorns
¼ teaspoon tarragon
⅛ teaspoon chervil
3 egg yolks
¾ cup butter, melted
½ teaspoon salt
¼ teaspoon paprika
1½ pounds ground beef

In the top part of a double boiler combine the wine, vinegar, shallots or scallions, peppercorns, tarragon and chervil. Cook until reduced almost by half. Strain, and return the liquid to the top of the double boiler. Cool. When cooled, place again over simmering water and alternately add the egg yolks and the butter, a little at a time, beating steadily. Cook until the sauce is slightly thickened. Add salt and paprika. Meanwhile, form the beef into 5 large patties and broil to desired doneness. Pour the sauce over the hamburgers. Makes 5 servings.

# Hamburger Steak with Yorkshire Pudding

2 pounds ground beef
Salt and pepper
Yorkshire Pudding (see below)

Shape the meat into a large steak about 1½ inches thick. Put it in the center of a large, heavy roasting pan. Brown the meat in a very hot oven, 500° F., 8 minutes for rare, 10 minutes for medium. Remove the meat from the oven and season with salt and pepper. Add some beef drippings or oil to make about ⅓ cup liquid in the bottom of the pan. Return the meat to the oven. When the drippings are hot, pour Yorkshire Pudding mixture around the meat. Reduce the heat to 475° F. and bake for about 20 minutes longer, or until the pudding is puffy and brown. Makes 6–7 servings.

YORKSHIRE PUDDING

2 eggs
1 cup milk
1 cup flour
¼ teaspoon salt

Beat the eggs and milk together well. Add the flour and salt and beat well.

# Steak Tartare

*Try serving Steak Tartare as a lovely luncheon dish. Since the meat is not cooked, be sure that it is lean and very fresh.*

1½ pounds freshly ground lean round or sirloin steak
   ( make sure butcher grinds beef twice )
½ cup minced onion
1 heaping tablespoon chopped capers
6 flat anchovy fillets, chopped fine or mashed
4 egg yolks
Thin onion rings
Whole capers
Salt and freshly ground black pepper
Watercress, carrot curls, cherry tomatoes, pickled gherkins
Pumpernickel or rye bread or white toast

Mix the meat, onion, capers and anchovies and shape the mixture into 4 or 5 round steaks, handling the meat as little as possible. Make an indentation in the center of each steak and drop in a raw egg yolk. Cover with onion rings and sprinkle with whole capers, salt and pepper. Garnish with watercress, carrot curls, cherry tomatoes and pickled gherkins. Serve with pumpernickel or rye bread or with white toast. Makes 4–5 servings.

# Savory Broiled Hamburger Ring

Parsley Butter (see below)
2½ pounds ground beef
1 cup fine soft bread crumbs
¼ cup chili sauce
¾ cup beef broth
1 tablespoon minced onion
1½ teaspoons salt
¼ teaspoon pepper
Paprika
8 servings (about 4 cups) hot cooked julienne-cut carrots

Prepare Parsley Butter and chill. In a large bowl combine the beef, bread crumbs, chili sauce, broth, onion, salt and pepper and mix lightly. Put the mixture on a round broiler-proof platter or casserole dish (not glass) and shape it into a ring about 10-inches in diameter, with an opening in the center about 4 inches in diameter. Sprinkle lightly with paprika. Broil 6 inches from the heat for 12 minutes, or until desired doneness. Fill the center with some of the carrots and serve the remainder of the carrots in a heated serving dish. Cut the meat into 8 wedges and top each with a slice of Parsley Butter. Makes 8 servings

PARSLEY BUTTER

½ cup butter, softened
⅓ cup finely chopped parsley
1 teaspoon lemon juice

Mix all ingredients well and shape into a roll on a piece of wet waxed paper. Wrap the roll in the paper and chill. Just before serving cut into 8 slices.

# Giant Teriyaki-Style Hamburger with Snow Peas

1½ pounds ground beef
Soy sauce
⅛ cup sherry
1 tablespoon honey
1 small clove garlic, crushed
¼ teaspoon ground ginger
1 small green pepper, in strips
1 small sweet red pepper, in strips
½ cup water chestnuts, halved
2 cups fresh or frozen snow peas
Salt
Hot cooked rice

In a broiling pan shape the beef into one large oval patty about 1¼ inches thick. Mix ¼ cup soy sauce, the sherry, honey, garlic and ginger and brush this on the patty while it is broiling to desired doneness. Arrange the pepper slices and water chestnuts in a separate broiling pan and pour the remaining soy sauce mixture over the top. Broil the vegetables for about 5 minutes, or until tender yet crisp. Meanwhile, boil the snow peas in a small amount of salted water for 8 minutes, less if using frozen peas. Vegetables should be just tender; do not overcook. When the patty is broiled to desired doneness, transfer it to a platter and surround it with the vegetables. Serve with rice and a pitcher of soy sauce. Makes 4–5 servings.

# Ground Beef Chop Suey

1 pound ground beef
2 medium onions, sliced thin
1 cup diagonally sliced celery
¼ pound mushrooms, sliced
3 tablespoons soy sauce
1 teaspoon ground ginger
1 teaspoon sugar
1 can ( 16 ounces ) bean sprouts, drained
1 beef bouillon cube dissolved in ¾ cup boiling water
   and cooled
1 tablespoon cornstarch
Hot cooked rice

In a skillet sauté the beef, onions and celery until the meat is browned, stirring to keep it crumbly. Pour off excess fat. Add the mushrooms, soy sauce, ginger and sugar. Cook for 2 minutes. Stir in the bean sprouts. Stir together the bouillon and cornstarch. Add to the beef mixture. Bring to a boil and cook for 1 minute, stirring constantly. Serve with rice. Makes 6 servings.

## Grecian Hamburgers

1½–2 pounds ground beef
1 medium onion, chopped fine
Salt and freshly ground black pepper
2 tablespoons chili sauce
Flour
12 medium-thick slices eggplant
Butter
1 cup Tomato Sauce (p. 263)

Mix the beef with the onion, 1 teaspoon salt, ½ teaspoon pepper and the chili sauce. Form into 6 flat cakes. Flour the eggplant slices and brown lightly in the butter. Season with salt and pepper to taste and keep warm while you broil or panfry the hamburgers quickly. Place a patty between 2 slices of eggplant and serve with Tomato Sauce. Makes 6 servings.

## Three-Decker Hamburgers

*Serve these with broiled tomatoes on the side. The tomatoes add color and are a wonderful complement to the meal.*

1 Spanish onion
1 medium eggplant
Milk
Cornmeal
Oil
1½ pounds ground beef
Salt and pepper

Slice the onion in ½-inch-thick slices. Slice the eggplant about ¾ of an inch thick. Dip the slices in milk and then cornmeal. Fry them in a little hot oil until tender and browned. Form the meat into 6 patties; broil or panfry to desired doneness and season with salt and pepper. On each plate pile eggplant, onion and hamburger. Makes 6 servings.

## Italian Beef Rolls

¼ pound ground beef
½ cup chopped hard salami
½ cup freshly grated Parmesan cheese
¼ cup fine dry bread crumbs
¼ cup minced parsley
2 hard-cooked eggs, chopped coarse
4 cloves garlic, crushed
½ teaspoon oregano
1½ cups beef broth
1 pound (about 3 pieces) round steak, ¼ inch thick,
   pounded very thin
2 tablespoons olive oil
¼ cup dry red wine
Tomato Mayonnaise, optional (see next page)

In a large bowl combine the ground beef, salami, cheese, bread crumbs, parsley, eggs, 3 cloves of the garlic, oregano and enough broth (about 1 cup) to make a soft mixture. Divide the mixture among the steak pieces and spread evenly. Roll up each piece jelly-roll fashion and tuck in the ends as much as possible. Tie each roll at both ends with kitchen twine and set aside. In a medium skillet over medium heat sauté the remaining clove of garlic in hot oil. Add the beef rolls and brown quickly on all sides. When browned, pour in the remaining broth and the wine. Cover and simmer gently for about 30 minutes, or until rolls are fork-tender. Lift out and cool. When ready to serve, remove the strings and slice the beef thin. If desired, reserve some broth to serve as gravy with the beef rolls or serve the rolls with Tomato Mayonnaise. Makes 6 servings.

TOMATO MAYONNAISE

1 cup mayonnaise
1 can (8 ounces) tomatoes (puréed with 1 roasted pepper or pimiento)
1 clove garlic, crushed

In a small bowl combine all the ingredients. Cover and chill for 30 minutes. Makes about 2 cups.

## Hamburger, Pizza Style

*Cut this into wedges and serve with buttery slices of zucchini.*

1½ pounds ground beef
Salt and pepper
1 cup Tomato Sauce (p. 263)
1 teaspoon oregano
6 flat anchovy fillets, chopped
1 package (8 ounces) mozzarella cheese
3 hot Italian sausages, sliced and sautéed
3 tablespoons freshly grated Parmesan cheese
Sliced stuffed olives and chopped parsley

Pat the meat out into a circle about ¾ of an inch thick on a baking sheet lined with foil. Sprinkle with salt and pepper. Broil almost to desired doneness; do not turn. Remove the meat from the broiler and spread with Tomato Sauce. Sprinkle with oregano and anchovy. Top with slices of mozzarella cheese and sausage slices. Sprinkle with Parmesan cheese. Broil until the cheese melts and browns. Garnish with olives and parsley. Makes 6 servings.

# Beef Patties Parmigiana

1½ pounds ground beef
1 teaspoon salt
¼ teaspoon pepper
1 egg, slightly beaten
2 tablespoons milk
Fine dry bread crumbs
3 tablespoons butter
1 cup Tomato Sauce (p. 263)
4–5 slices mozzarella cheese
Freshly grated Parmesan cheese

Mix the beef, salt and pepper together well, handling the meat as little as possible. Shape into 4 or 5 patties. Mix the egg and milk. Dip the patties in the mixture, then in the bread crumbs. Brown on both sides in the butter in a broiler-proof skillet. Pour the Tomato Sauce over the patties, top each with a slice of mozzarella and sprinkle with Parmesan. Put under the broiler until the mozzarella melts. Makes 4–5 servings.

# Eggplant Parmigiana

1 pound ground beef
½ cup olive oil
2 cups Tomato Sauce (p. 263), heated
1 medium to large eggplant
Flour
Salt and pepper
1 cup freshly grated Parmesan cheese
½ pound mozzarella cheese, sliced thin

In a skillet sauté the beef in 1 tablespoon of the olive oil, stirring with a fork, until all the red color is gone. Pour off the excess fat and add the meat to the Tomato Sauce, stirring well. Cover and simmer while preparing the eggplant. Peel the eggplant and cut it into ¼-inch-thick slices. Dip each slice in flour lightly seasoned with salt and pepper. Heat 2 tablespoons of the oil in a large skillet and brown each eggplant slice on both sides. As they become browned, transfer them with a wide spatula to a platter. Brown all the slices, adding more oil when necessary. Put a layer of eggplant in the bottom of a lightly oiled shallow baking dish. Cover with a layer of meat sauce. Sprinkle with Parmesan and cover with mozzarella slices. Repeat, ending with a layer of mozzarella. Bake in a preheated 375° F. oven for 25 minutes. Makes 4–6 servings.

# Moussaka

*It isn't often that one pound of ground beef will suffice for eight people, but it will with this variation of a famous Greek specialty. This dish can be baked—even frozen—in advance, except for the creamy topping that is added at the end.*

½ pound mushrooms, sliced
Butter
3 cups onion rings
Olive oil
1 pound ground beef
Salt and pepper
¼ cup red wine
1 medium to large eggplant
3 eggs
¾ cup flour
2 cups Tomato Sauce (p. 263)
1 cup cream
2 tablespoons chopped parsley

Sauté the mushrooms in 2 tablespoons of butter until all the moisture has disappeared, stirring occasionally. Transfer the mushrooms to a plate. Sauté the onion rings in 2 tablespoons of olive oil in the same skillet until soft but not brown; remove to another plate. Cook the meat in the same skillet, adding 1 teaspoon of salt and ¼ teaspoon of pepper and stirring with a fork to break up the meat. When the meat is lightly browned, pour off the excess fat and transfer it to a bowl. Rinse the pan out with the wine, then pour this over the meat. Peel and slice the eggplant in ½-inch-thick slices. Beat 1 of the eggs with 1 tablespoon of water in a shallow soup plate. On another plate spread the flour mixed with 1 teaspoon of salt and a little pepper. Dip each slice of eggplant first in the egg and then in the flour, coating both sides. Sauté in butter until lightly browned on both sides. Put ½ cup of the Tomato Sauce in the bottom of a deep 2½-quart casserole. Cover with a layer of eggplant, a layer of mushrooms, a layer of onions, a layer of meat and a layer of sauce. Repeat until everything is used, ending with a layer of sauce. Cover and bake in a preheated 375° F. oven for 40 minutes. Just before serving, beat the remaining 2 eggs and the cream with ½ teaspoon salt, ⅛ teaspoon pepper and the chopped parsley. Pour over the top and bake for 10 minutes, or until set. Makes 8 servings.

## Ground Beef and Eggplant Skillet

1 pound ground beef
1 clove garlic, halved
1 medium eggplant, peeled, in ½-inch cubes
2 green peppers, in ½-inch chunks
1 onion, quartered and sliced
1 can (16 ounces) tomatoes, undrained
1 teaspoon each salt and basil
½ teaspoon oregano
Freshly ground black pepper

In a large skillet brown the beef and garlic lightly, breaking up the meat with a fork as it cooks; drain off excess fat and discard the garlic. Add the eggplant, stir and cook over low heat for about 10 minutes. Add the green peppers, onion, tomatoes and seasonings. Cover and cook over low heat for 25 minutes, or until the mixture is well blended. Makes 4 servings.

## Beef-Stuffed Eggplant

1 eggplant, about 1½ pounds
Salt
3 tablespoons oil
½ cup finely chopped onion
1 pound ground beef
½ cup chopped green pepper
2 tablespoons chopped parsley
⅛ teaspoon allspice
½ cup Tomato Sauce (p. 263)
Pepper
1 tablespoon fine dry bread crumbs
2 tablespoons freshly grated Parmesan cheese

Cut eggplant in half lengthwise. Make several cuts in the pulp and sprinkle with salt. Let stand for about 20 minutes. Put the oil in a large, heavy kettle and add the eggplant halves, cut side down. Cover and cook for about 10 minutes. Turn and cook for 5 minutes longer, or until tender. Put in a shallow dish; cool slightly. Scoop out the pulp and dice it. Cook the onion and meat, stirring, until the meat loses its red color. Drain off excess fat. Add the eggplant pulp and the green pepper, parsley, allspice and Tomato Sauce. Cook all together, stirring often, for about

5 minutes. Season to taste with salt and pepper. Fill the eggplant shells with this mixture and top with bread crumbs mixed with Parmesan cheese. Bake in a preheated 375° F. oven for 20 minutes, or until hot and lightly browned. Makes 6 servings.

## Stuffed Zucchini

4–5 medium zucchini, each about 6 inches long
Salt
¾ cup finely chopped onion
1 small clove garlic, minced
3 tablespoons olive oil
¼ pound Italian sausage, casing removed
½ pound ground beef
¼ teaspoon pepper
1 teaspoon rosemary, crumbled
3 slices bread
½ cup milk
3 tablespoons freshly grated Parmesan cheese
¼ cup chopped parsley

Cut off the ends of the zucchini. Cook the zucchini whole in lightly salted boiling water for 8 minutes, or until just tender. Drain and cool slightly. Cut them in half lengthwise, remove some of the pulp and reserve. Cook the onion and garlic in the oil in a skillet for about 2 minutes (do not brown). Add the broken sausage meat, beef, ½ teaspoon salt, the pepper and rosemary and cook over low heat, stirring often, for about 15 minutes. Drain off excess fat. Soak the bread in the milk, break it up and squeeze out some of the milk if necessary. Add to the meat mixture along with the cheese, zucchini pulp and chopped parsley; mix well. Stuff the zucchini shells and put them in an oiled baking dish. Bake in a preheated 325° F. oven for 25 minutes. Makes 4–5 servings.

# Zucchini and Hamburger Casserole

4 medium zucchini, sliced
1 teaspoon salt
1 pound ground beef
½ cup chopped onion
1 clove garlic, minced or crushed
¼ teaspoon each oregano, basil, thyme and pepper
2 cups cooked rice
1 cup Tomato Sauce (p. 263)
1 cup cottage cheese
¾ cup shredded sharp Cheddar cheese
1 egg

Toss the zucchini with the salt. Place half in a greased 2-quart casserole. Sauté the beef, onion, garlic and spices in a skillet, breaking up the meat with a fork, until the meat is browned. Pour off excess fat. Stir in the rice and Tomato Sauce. Spread the meat mixture over the zucchini in the casserole. Mix the cottage cheese, ½ cup of the Cheddar cheese and the egg; spoon this over the meat mixture. Layer with the remaining zucchini and sprinkle with the remaining Cheddar. Bake in a preheated 350° F. oven for 20–25 minutes, or until bubbly. Makes 6 servings.

# Hamburger and Lima Bean Casserole

2 cups fresh or 1 package (10 ounces) frozen lima beans
2 tablespoons butter
Salt and pepper
½ teaspoon marjoram
1½ cups soft bread crumbs
¼ cup milk
1 egg, beaten
1 clove garlic, minced
½ cup chopped water chestnuts
1 pound ground beef
1 cup beef broth
1 cup sour cream
Paprika

Cook the beans in unsalted water until tender. Drain and season with 1 tablespoon of the butter, salt and pepper to taste and marjoram. At the same time soak the bread crumbs in the milk for 3 minutes. Add to the bread crumbs the egg, garlic, three-quarters of the water chestnuts and all the beef. Mix well and shape into 1½-inch balls. Heat the remaining tablespoon of butter in a heavy skillet and sauté half the balls for 4–5 minutes, shaking the pan frequently. Transfer the balls to a 2-quart casserole and repeat with the other half of the balls. Add the broth to the pan drippings and stir until blended. Pour this over the meatballs. Add the lima beans and bake for 30 minutes in preheated 350° F. oven. Spread the sour cream and the remaining water chestnuts over the top and cook for 5 minutes more. Sprinkle with paprika and serve. Makes 4 servings.

# Broccoli and Hamburger Casserole

1 tablespoon butter
1 pound ground beef
1 large bunch broccoli or 2 packages ( 10 ounces each )
   frozen broccoli, in florets
2 eggs
1 cup cream
¾ teaspoon salt
½ teaspoon white pepper
½ teaspoon nutmeg
¾ cup grated Cheddar cheese

Heat the butter in a skillet; add the beef and cook until its red color disappears, stirring frequently to break up the meat. Then spread the beef in a shallow casserole. Meanwhile cook the broccoli until just tender and put florets in the casserole with the meat. Beat the eggs. Mix well with the cream, seasonings and cheese. Pour this mixture over the broccoli and bake for 40 minutes in a preheated 350° F. oven. Makes 4–5 servings.

# Ground Beef and Green Beans, Chinese Style

1 large onion, sliced very thin
1 clove garlic, crushed
1 tablespoon butter
1½ pounds ground beef
3 cups water
Soy sauce
1½ pounds fresh green beans
1 cup water chestnuts, sliced
2½ tablespoons cornstarch
Hot cooked rice

Brown the onion and garlic in the butter in a large skillet. Add the meat and stir, breaking it up with a fork, until browned; pour off excess fat. Add the water blended with 3 tablespoons of the soy sauce. Stir well, and bring to a boil. Add the beans and water chestnuts, cover and simmer for 10 minutes. Blend the cornstarch with 2 tablespoons of water and add to the contents of the skillet. Stir until the mixture thickens. Serve on heated plates with side bowls of rice. Have a small pitcher of soy sauce on the table. Makes 6 servings.

# Mushroom, Ground Beef and Green Bean Casserole

*Nutritious and filling.*

1 tablespoon oil
1 cup chopped onion
½ pound mushrooms, sliced
1 pound ground beef
1 teaspoon salt
¼ teaspoon pepper
1 teaspoon basil, crumbled
1 cup beef broth
2 tablespoons tomato paste
1 pound cut green beans
2 cups mashed potatoes
1 tablespoon freshly grated Parmesan cheese

Heat the oil in a large skillet. Sauté the onion until it is transparent. Add the mushrooms, beef and seasonings. Cook, stirring frequently, until the meat is browned; pour off excess fat. Add the broth and tomato paste. Simmer for a few minutes, then add the green beans. Pour into a shallow 2-quart broiler-proof baking dish. Spread the mashed potatoes on top and sprinkle with cheese. Put under the broiler until lightly browned. Makes 6 servings.

# Meatball-Mushroom-Broccoli Stew

¼ pound mushrooms, sliced
2 tablespoons butter
2 cups beef broth
1 pound ground beef
2 tablespoons cold water
1 teaspoon salt
¼ teaspoon pepper
1 cup broken uncooked spaghetti
3 cups 2-inch pieces broccoli florets and stems ( ½ bunch )
Freshly grated Parmesan cheese

In a Dutch oven sauté the mushrooms in the butter until golden. Add the broth and bring to a boil. Combine the beef, water, salt and pepper. Shape into walnut-size meatballs and drop into the simmering broth; simmer for 10 minutes. Stir in the spaghetti, cover and cook for 10 minutes. Add the broccoli, cover and cook for 10 minutes, or until the broccoli and spaghetti are tender. Adjust the seasonings. Sprinkle with Parmesan cheese. Makes 4 servings.

# Hamburger-Egg-Spinach Dish

1 large onion, chopped
5 tablespoons butter
1 pound ground beef
1 package (10 ounces) frozen spinach
1½ teaspoons salt
1 teaspoon oregano
¼ teaspoon pepper
6 eggs, slightly beaten
½ cup sour cream

Cook the onion in the butter in a large skillet until golden brown. Add the beef and sauté, stirring to break up the lumps, until the meat loses its red color. Pour off excess fat. Cook the spinach as directed on the package; slightly drain. Add to the meat mixture along with the seasonings and cook for a few minutes, or until most of the liquid has evaporated. Add the eggs and scramble them until they are of desired doneness. Stir in the sour cream and serve at once. Makes 4–6 servings.

# Stove-Top Beef-Stuffed Red or Green Peppers

*Buy chunky peppers with flat bottoms for these.*

4–5 medium green or red peppers
1 pound ground beef
¼ cup finely chopped onion
1 cup soft bread crumbs
¼ teaspoon prepared horseradish
½ teaspoon dry mustard
1 teaspoon salt
¼ teaspoon seasoned pepper
2 tablespoons catsup
1 egg, slightly beaten
¼ cup milk
Parsley

Cut off the stem ends of the peppers and remove the seeds. Mix the remaining ingredients, except for the parsley. Fill the peppers with the meat mixture. Place them in a deep kettle with about 1 inch of water. Cover and simmer, adding a little more water if necessary, for 45 minutes, or until the meat is done. Garnish with sprigs of parsley. Makes 4–5 servings.

# Beef-Stuffed Peppers with Cheese Sauce

4 green peppers
Salt
5 tablespoons butter
1 pound ground beef
1 small onion, sliced
Pepper
¼ cup whole wheat (or white) flour
2 cups milk
1 cup diced Cheddar cheese

Split the peppers lengthwise and remove seeds. Parboil the peppers in a small amount of boiling salted water for about 5 minutes. Drain well. In a skillet melt 1 tablespoon of the butter and cook the beef and onion, breaking up the meat with a fork, until the meat loses its red color; pour off excess fat. Add 1 teaspoon salt and a dash of pepper. Fill the peppers with the mixture and arrange them in a shallow baking dish. Melt the remaining butter and blend in the flour. Gradually add the milk and cook, stirring, until thickened. Stir in the cheese and season to taste. Pour sauce over the peppers and bake in a preheated 350° F. oven for about 30 minutes. Makes 4 servings.

## Creole Stuffed Peppers

4 large green peppers
1 pound ground beef
2 cups cooked rice
Salt and pepper
3½ cups Creole Sauce (p. 267)

Split the peppers lengthwise and remove the seeds. Parboil
the peppers for 5 minutes; drain. Cook the beef, stirring
frequently, until it loses its red color. Pour off excess fat.
Mix the beef, rice, seasonings, and ¼ cup Creole Sauce.
Pack the peppers with the mixture. Put them in a large,
shallow baking dish. Pour about three-quarters of the
remaining sauce around the peppers. Cover; bake in a
preheated 350° F. oven for 45 minutes. Serve with the remaining sauce, heated. Makes 8 servings.

## Country-Style Beef and Potato Casserole

2 slices bacon, diced
4 medium potatoes, peeled and sliced thin
1 teaspoon salt
¼ teaspoon pepper
2 tablespoons butter
1 pound ground beef
1 medium onion, chopped
1½ cups Tomato-Meat Sauce (p. 265)

Cook the bacon until crisp and browned; pour off excess fat. Add the potatoes, cover and cook slowly for 10 minutes, stirring occasionally. Sprinkle with ½ teaspoon of the salt and ⅛ teaspoon of the pepper and put in a shallow 1½-quart baking dish. Melt the butter in the same skillet and add the beef and onion. Cook until the beef loses its red color, breaking it up with a fork; drain excess fat. Add the remaining salt and pepper and put the meat mixture on top of the potatoes. Cover with Tomato-Meat Sauce. Bake in a preheated 350° F. oven for about 45 minutes. Makes 4–6 servings.

# Beef-Stuffed Baked Potatoes

1 pound ground beef
6 tablespoons butter
¾ teaspoon salt
¼ teaspoon pepper
6 medium potatoes, baked
Milk
1 small onion, minced
¼ teaspoon garlic powder
1 tablespoon chopped parsley
2 stalks celery, chopped fine
¾ pound or more Cheddar cheese, shredded

Brown the beef in 1 tablespoon of the butter in a skillet, breaking it up with a fork as it cooks. Add the salt and pepper; drain off excess fat and set aside. Cut the baked potatoes in half lengthwise and scoop out the insides into a large bowl. Mash the potatoes and add the remaining butter and enough milk to moisten. Beat well, then add the beef and the remaining ingredients. Fill the potato shells with the mixture and place them on a baking sheet. Top each with more Cheddar cheese if desired and bake in a preheated 400° F. oven for about 15 minutes. Makes 6 servings.

# Bulgarian Potato-Beef Moussaka

5 medium potatoes, peeled and in ¾-inch slices
Salt
½ cup chopped onion
2 tablespoons butter
1 pound ground beef
¼ cup dry white or red table wine
½ cup Tomato Sauce (p. 263)
1 tablespoon chopped parsley
½ teaspoon paprika
¼ teaspoon pepper
2 medium tomatoes, sliced
2 tablespoons flour
2 egg yolks
1 cup plain yogurt
½ cup shredded sharp Cheddar cheese

Boil the potatoes until they are almost done. Drain them and sprinkle with salt. Sauté the onion in the butter in a skillet. Add the meat and brown, stirring frequently with a fork; drain off excess fat. Mix the wine, Tomato Sauce, parsley, paprika, pepper and 1 teaspoon salt and add this to the meat; simmer for 10 minutes. Make a layer of half the potato slices in a greased, shallow 1½-quart baking dish. Add all the meat sauce and a second layer of potato. Top with tomato slices. Beat the flour, egg yolks and yogurt together and pour this over the tomato slices. Sprinkle with Cheddar cheese and bake in a preheated 375° F. oven for 30 minutes. Makes 4–6 servings.

# Hamburger Casserole à la Grecque

2 pounds ground beef
4 medium onions, chopped
3 cloves garlic, minced
1½ teaspoons salt
¼ teaspoon pepper
1½ cups beef broth
1 can (6 or 7 ounces) tomato paste
½ cup dry red table wine
1 pound potatoes, peeled and diced
3 bay leaves
3-inch stick cinnamon

In a large skillet cook the meat, onion, garlic, salt and pepper. Stir frequently, breaking the meat up with a fork, until the meat loses its red color; drain off excess fat. Add the remaining ingredients and bring to a boil. Put in a casserole, cover and bake in a preheated 350° F. oven for about 1¼ hours, or until the potatoes are done. Remove cinnamon stick. Makes 6 servings.

# Farmer's Pride

3 large potatoes, peeled
2 large onions, peeled
1 large green pepper, seeded
1 crisp apple, peeled and cored
1¾ pounds ground beef
¼ pound pork sausage meat
¼ cup finely crushed soda crackers
¼ cup evaporated milk
2 teaspoons salt
¼ teaspoon pepper
2 eggs, slightly beaten
1 cup Tomato Sauce (p. 263)

Force the potatoes, onions, green pepper and apple through a food chopper, using a coarse blade. Mix lightly but thoroughly with the remaining ingredients except the Tomato Sauce. Pack into a 9-by-5-by-3-inch loaf pan or a shallow 2-quart baking dish. Cover with Tomato Sauce. Bake in a preheated 350° F. oven for about 1½ hours. Makes 6–8 servings.

# Hamburger Harvest Casserole

*Drained canned whole-kernel corn and drained canned tomatoes may be used instead of fresh.*

1 onion, chopped
2 green peppers, sliced
¼ cup butter
1 pound ground beef
1½ teaspoons salt
¼ teaspoon pepper
2 cups cut fresh corn
4 tomatoes, sliced
½ cup soft bread crumbs

Brown the onion and peppers in the butter Add the meat, breaking it up with a fork, and cook for a few minutes, or until the meat loses its red color. Season with salt and pepper. In a 2-quart casserole arrange layers of half the corn, meat and tomatoes. Repeat. Cover with crumbs. Bake in a preheated 350° F. oven for about 35 minutes. Makes 4 servings.

# Beef Casserole with Corn Topping

2 tablespoons butter
1 medium onion, minced
2 pounds ground beef
2 tablespoons flour
2–3 tablespoons chili powder
3 teaspoons salt
¼ teaspoon pepper
½ cup water
2 hard-cooked eggs, in eighths
1 can (17 ounces) cream-style corn
2 eggs, well beaten
1 cup milk

Melt the butter in a hot skillet and cook the onion for about 2–3 minutes. Add the beef and, stirring frequently, cook until the meat loses its red color. Drain off excess fat. Mix the flour, chili powder, 2 teaspoons of the salt and the pepper with water and stir into the meat mixture. Cook, stirring, until thickened. Remove from heat and fold in the hard-cooked eggs; put in a 3-quart casserole. In a saucepan, combine the corn, remaining salt, the beaten eggs and the milk; cook over medium heat, stirring until thickened. Pour this over the mixture in the casserole. Bake in a preheated 350° F. oven for 30–40 minutes. Makes 6–8 servings.

# Spanish Skillet Supper

*A super-easy supper dish. Serve over big helpings of rice.*

1 pound ground beef
1 medium onion, chopped
1 small green pepper, chopped
1 can (16 ounces) tomatoes, undrained
3 tablespoons catsup
1 tablespoon Worcestershire sauce
½ teaspoon hot pepper sauce
1 teaspoon salt

Brown the meat lightly in a skillet, breaking it up with a fork as it cooks. Drain off the excess fat. Add the onion and green pepper and cook, stirring, until tender. Stir in ¼ cup water and the remaining ingredients until well blended. Cover and simmer for about 30 minutes. Makes 4–6 servings.

# Acapulco Casserole

½–1 pound ground beef
1 cup chopped onion
1 cup chopped celery
1 clove garlic, pressed
1½ tablespoons Worcestershire sauce
1 teaspoon chili powder
1 can (16 ounces) red kidney beans, drained
1 can (16 ounces) cream-style corn
1 cup Tomato Sauce (p. 263)
6 tortillas
½ cup shredded Cheddar cheese

Brown the meat in a large skillet, stirring frequently with a fork to break it up; drain off excess fat. Add the remaining ingredients, except tortillas and cheese. Cook, stirring, for 3 minutes. Put 1 tortilla in a round 2-quart casserole and top with 1 cup of the sauce mixture. Top with another tortilla, then 1 cup sauce. Continue until all the tortillas are used. Top with the remaining sauce and sprinkle with cheese. Bake, uncovered, in a preheated 350° F. oven for about 30 minutes. Makes 6–8 servings.

# Taco Casserole

*Either buy tortillas, or make your own (see recipe p. 135).*

1 tablespoon oil
1 pound ground beef
¾ cup chopped scallions (green onion)
1 clove garlic, minced
1 can (10½ ounces) condensed beef consommé
½ cup Sauterne
1 can (12 ounces) Mexican-style corn
1 can (6 ounces) tomato paste
1 tablespoon chili powder
½ teaspoon cumin
4 drops hot pepper sauce
Salt
3 tortillas, each torn in sixths
¾ cup shredded sharp Cheddar cheese
1 cup shredded lettuce
1 large avocado, sliced thin
1 medium tomato, sliced very thin

Heat the oil in a skillet, add the beef, ½ cup of the scallions and the garlic and sauté, breaking up the meat with a fork, until the onions are limp. Drain off excess fat. Add the consommé and wine and bring to a boil. Simmer for 1 minute, then add the corn, tomato paste, chili powder, cumin and pepper sauce and mix well. Add salt to taste and pour into a 9-by-9-by-2-inch baking dish. Poke the tortilla pieces into the meat mixture and bake, uncovered, in a preheated 350° F. over for about 25 minutes.

Remove from the oven and sprinkle with cheese. Then top with the remaining scallions, the lettuce, avocado and tomato. Serve at once. Makes 4–6 servings.

# Beef Tamale Casserole

1½ pounds ground beef
¼ cup olive oil or vegetable shortening
1 cup chopped onion
1 clove garlic, minced
½ cup chopped green pepper
3 cans (8 ounces each) tomatoes
1 can (16 ounces) whole-kernel corn
1 tablespoon salt
1½ teaspoons chili powder
¼ teaspoon pepper
½ cup yellow cornmeal
1 cup pitted whole ripe olives
Topping (see next page)

Brown the beef in the oil in a skillet, breaking it up with a fork as it cooks. Drain off excess fat. Add the onion, garlic and green pepper and cook for 2–3 minutes. Stir in the tomatoes, corn and seasonings and simmer for about 5 minutes. In a bowl mix the cornmeal and 1 cup of water. Stir this into the meat mixture, cover and cook slowly for about 10 minutes. Add the olives and pour into a shallow 2½-quart baking dish. Pour the Topping mixture around the edge of the dish and bake in a preheated 375° F. oven for about 20 minutes. Makes 6 servings.

TOPPING

1½ cups milk
1 teaspoon salt
2 tablespoons butter
½ cup yellow cornmeal
1 cup grated sharp Cheddar cheese
2 eggs, slightly beaten

Heat the milk, salt and butter in a heavy saucepan. Gradually stir in the cornmeal and cook, stirring, until thickened. Remove from the heat and stir in the Cheddar cheese. Then stir in the eggs.

## Mexican Tortilla Sandwiches

1 pound ground beef
1 large onion, chopped
2 small cloves garlic, minced
2 cups Tomato Sauce (p. 263)
Salt and pepper
Freshly grated Parmesan cheese
1½ cups yellow cornmeal
1½ cups flour
2 eggs
Oil
1 jar (4 ounces) green chilies, drained
Shredded Cheddar cheese
Raw onion rings
Shredded lettuce

Cook the beef, breaking it up with a fork, in a skillet until it loses its red color. Drain off excess fat. Add chopped onion and garlic and cook for 5 minutes longer. Add 1 cup of the Tomato Sauce, 1 teaspoon salt and ¼ teaspoon pepper and simmer for a few minutes. Add ½ cup Parmesan cheese and set aside. Mix the cornmeal, flour and eggs with 2½ cups water and season with salt and pepper. Shape into very thin flat cakes like tortillas, about 7 inches in diameter, and cook on both sides in a little oil until done. Put half of them in 5 or 6 greased individual serving dishes or pie pans. Divide the filling among the tortillas. Chop the chilies and sprinkle them on top of the filling. Top with the remaining tortillas, cover with remaining sauce and sprinkle with Cheddar cheese. Cover with foil and bake in a preheated 400° F. oven for 15 minutes, or until piping hot. Top with onion rings and lettuce and pass extra Parmesan cheese. Makes 5–6 servings.

# Beef Enchiladas

**Oil**
**½ cup chopped onion**
**1 pound ground beef**
**1 clove garlic, crushed**
**1 cup Tomato Sauce (p. 263)**
**¾ teaspoon oregano**
**½ teaspoon salt**
**¼–½ teaspoon crushed red pepper**
**12 Tortillas (see recipe p. 135)**
**3 cups shredded Cheddar cheese**
**Enchilada Sauce (see next page)**

Heat 1 tablespoon oil in a skillet; add the onion and cook until tender. Add the meat and garlic and cook, stirring, until lightly browned. Drain off excess fat, and add the Tomato Sauce, oregano, salt, and red pepper and cook, stirring constantly, until thickened, for about 5 minutes. Fry the tortillas one at a time in about 2 tablespoons hot oil in a skillet, turning once, for 1 minute, or until softened. Drain well on paper towels. Spread each tortilla with about 2 tablespoons of the meat mixture and sprinkle lightly with some of the Cheddar cheese. Roll the tortillas up and arrange them, side by side, seam side down, in a greased 13-by-9-by-2-inch baking dish. Spoon the Enchilada Sauce over the enchiladas, sprinkle with the remaining cheese and bake in a preheated 350° F. oven for 15–20 minutes, or until the sauce is bubbly. Makes 6 servings.

ENCHILADA SAUCE

2 cups Tomato Sauce (p. 263)
¼–½ teaspoon crushed red pepper
¼ teaspoon salt
1 clove garlic, crushed

Combine all the ingredients in a saucepan and heat to simmering.

# Picadillo

*A popular Cuban dish. Some prefer to leave out the tomatoes.*

3 garlic cloves, minced
1 large onion, chopped
2 tablespoons oil or butter
Salt and pepper
⅛ teaspoon rosemary
⅛ teaspoon ground ginger
1 pound ground beef, broken up
½ cup dry white table wine
2 large tomatoes, peeled and chopped
½ cup raisins (dark or light), plumped up in hot water
½ cup sliced pimiento-stuffed olives
1 green pepper, chopped
2 bananas, in eighths
1 teaspoon lemon juice

In a large skillet sauté the garlic and onion in oil, stirring frequently, for 5 minutes. Stir in the seasonings, meat and wine. Stir in the tomatoes, raisins and olives. Add the green pepper and cook until the pepper is hot but still retains color and crispness. Push the meat mixture to one side of the skillet and cook the banana slices for 3 minutes, turning each piece once. Sprinkle the bananas with lemon juice. Serve alongside the meat. Makes 3–5 servings.

## Savory Hamburger Stew

1 pound ground beef
1 tablespoon butter
1 onion, sliced
1½ teaspoons salt
¼ teaspoon pepper
1 tablespoon steak sauce
1 can (19 ounces) tomatoes
3 medium potatoes, peeled and sliced
3 medium carrots, sliced
2 stalks celery, diced
Split hot biscuits (optional)

Brown the beef lightly in the butter, stirring with a fork to
break it up. Drain off excess fat. Add the onion and cook
for a few minutes longer. Add the remaining ingredients,
except the biscuits. Bring to a boil and simmer, covered,
for 30 minutes, or until the vegetables are tender. Serve on
biscuits. Makes 4–6 servings.

## Hobo Stew

*A favorite with teen-agers. It can be made ahead and
reheated.*

1 cup thinly sliced onion
1 cup coarsely chopped green pepper
¼ cup olive oil
2 pounds ground beef
1 can (16 ounces) red kidney beans, drained
1 tablespoon steak sauce
1 can (16 ounces) whole-kernel corn, drained
1 can (35 ounces) Italian-style tomatoes
2 cups Tomato Sauce (p. 263)
Basil
Dry mustard
Salt and pepper

Cook the onion and green pepper in oil in a large skillet or kettle until the onion is golden. Add the beef and cook, stirring with a fork to break up the meat, until browned. Drain off excess fat. Add the remaining ingredients and mix well. Cover and simmer for 15–20 minutes. Makes 8–10 servings.

# Hamburger-Cabbage Stew

1½ pounds ground beef
1½ medium heads cabbage, chopped
2 tablespoons chopped green pepper
4 large carrots, sliced
3 stalks celery, chopped
3 teaspoons salt
¼ teaspoon pepper
½ cup uncooked rice or 1½ cups cooked

Cook the beef slowly in a kettle until it loses its red color, breaking it up with a fork. Drain off excess fat. Add 4 cups of water and the remaining ingredients, except the rice. Bring to a boil, cover and simmer for about 45 minutes. Cook the rice separately and add it to the mixture. Simmer for a few minutes longer. Makes 6 servings.

# Basic Directions for Cabbage Rolls

There are many different ways to cook cabbage rolls. We offer four favorite variations. Here are the basic directions for preparing the leaves.

Remove and discard the outer, wilted leaves of the cabbage. Using a sharp knife, cut out the center core. Put the cabbage in a kettle of lightly salted boiling water over high heat for 3–5 minutes, or until the leaves become loose and slightly limp. With tongs, remove the number of leaves the recipe calls for (usually 8–12). Always choose the largest leaves available. For some recipes you should reserve the cabbage liquid.

Always save the remaining cabbage to serve as a vegetable or in spicy Cabbage-Meatball Soup (p. 10).

# Old-fashioned Cabbage Rolls

1 cabbage, about 4 pounds
1 pound ground beef
½ pound ground pork
1 cup cooked rice (about ⅓ cup uncooked)
1 egg, slightly beaten
½ teaspoon garlic salt
¾ teaspoon salt
¼ teaspoon pepper
½ teaspoon nutmeg
1 cup chopped onion
¼ cup chopped parsley
Butter
1 cup Tomato Sauce (p. 263)
1 can (27 ounces) sauerkraut, drained
Sour cream (optional)

Prepare the cabbage as in the basic directions (p. 68), reserving the liquid and setting aside 12 large leaves. Shred the remaining cabbage. Lightly mix the meats, rice, egg and seasonings. Divide the filling among the leaves and make packages by folding in the sides. Sauté the onion and parsley in 2 tablespoons butter. Stir in the Tomato Sauce and 1 cup of the cabbage liquid. Pour half the tomato mixture into a Dutch oven. Put cabbage rolls into the Dutch oven, seam side down. Top with sauerkraut and shredded cabbage. Dot with 2 tablespoons butter and pour the remaining tomato mixture over all. Cover and simmer 2–2½ hours. Serve with sour cream if desired. Makes 6 servings.

# Swedish Cabbage Rolls

*These are good with lingonberries or cranberries.*

1 cabbage, about 3 pounds
Salt
1 cup cooked rice (about ⅓ cup uncooked)
1 pound ground beef
½ teaspoon nutmeg
1 small onion, grated
⅔ cup milk
¼ cup butter
1 tablespoon flour
1 cup light cream
Pepper

Prepare the cabbage as in the basic directions (p. 68), reserving the liquid and setting aside 12 outer leaves. Lightly mix 1 teaspoon salt and the rice, beef, nutmeg, onion and milk. Divide this filling among the leaves. Make packages, folding in the sides, and sauté them in the butter until well browned on both sides, beginning with seam side down. Pour 1 cup cabbage liquid over the top, cover and simmer for about 1 hour. Add more liquid if necessary. Remove the rolls to a hot serving dish. Blend together the flour and cream and stir this into the pan juices. Bring to a boil, stirring, and simmer for 2–3 minutes. Season with salt and pepper and pour over the cabbage rolls. Makes 6 servings.

# Creole Cabbage Rolls

1 cabbage, about 4 pounds
1 pound ground beef
1 cup cooked rice (about ⅓ cup uncooked)
¼ cup minced onion
¼ cup minced parsley
Salt and pepper
2–3 drops hot pepper sauce
1 egg
1 clove garlic, crushed
½ cup chopped onion
¼ cup chopped green pepper
2 tablespoons butter
1 can (16 ounces) tomatoes, undrained
1 tablespoon honey
1 beef bouillon cube
¼ cup lemon juice
¼ cup seedless raisins

Prepare the cabbage as in basic directions (p. 68), setting aside 12 outer leaves. Chop the remainder. Mix the beef, rice, minced onion, parsley, 1 teaspoon salt, ¼ teaspoon pepper, hot pepper sauce and egg. Divide this filling among the leaves and make packages, folding in sides. Put them, seam side down, in a 3-quart casserole. Sauté the garlic, chopped onion and green pepper in the butter for 2–3 minutes. Add ½ teaspoon each salt and pepper and the remaining ingredients. Simmer gently for 10 minutes, then spoon over the cabbage rolls. Cover and bake in a preheated 350° F. oven for about 1 hour. Steam the chopped cabbage, season and serve as a side dish with the rolls. Makes 6 servings.

# Sweet and Pungent
# Cabbage Rolls

*This is best when prepared a day or two before serving. Keep refrigerated, and then, one hour before serving, put the cabbage rolls and sauce in a shallow baking dish and heat, uncovered, in a preheated 300° F. oven for 1 hour.*

1 cabbage, about 2½ pounds
1 medium onion, sliced
1 apple, cored and sliced
⅓ cup uncooked rice
2 pounds ground beef
2 medium onions, grated
Salt
2 cups Tomato Sauce (p. 263)
¾ cup packed dark brown sugar
3 tablespoons lemon juice
½ teaspoon ground ginger
1 large bay leaf
2 whole allspice

Prepare the cabbage as in the basic directions (p. 68), setting aside 12–15 outer leaves. Use the remaining leaves to line a roasting pan, tucking the onion and apple slices under the leaves. Bring the rice to a boil in ¾ cup water and simmer for 5–7 minutes. Drain off the water and add the rice to the beef, along with the grated onion, 1 table-spoon salt and ¼ cup water. Mix well and put about 2 tablespoons of the mixture on each leaf. Make packages, folding in the sides. Put the rolls, seam side down, in the prepared pan. Bring ½ cup water, 1 teaspoon salt, the

Tomato Sauce, brown sugar, lemon juice and ginger to a boil and pour over the cabbage rolls. Cover and bake in a preheated 375° F. oven for about 1½ hours. Uncover, lower the heat to 325° F. and bake for 50 minutes longer. Add the bay leaf and allspice and bake for 10 minutes longer. Cool slightly and skim off the fat. Carefully remove the cabbage rolls to a warm platter. Press the sauce, vegetables and apple through a food mill or strainer. Reheat and pour over the cabbage rolls. Makes 6–7 servings.

# Stuffed Spanish Omelet for Two

4 slices bacon
1 small onion, chopped
1 stalk celery, chopped
4 mushrooms, chopped
⅓ pound ground beef
½ cup Tomato Sauce (p. 263)
4 eggs
Salt and pepper
1 teaspoon oil

Fry the bacon until crisp. Remove the bacon to paper toweling to drain, and break it into small pieces. Cook the onion and celery in the bacon fat until the onion is lightly browned. Add the mushrooms and beef and cook for 2 minutes, stirring with a fork. Drain off excess fat. Add the Tomato Sauce, cover and simmer for 10 minutes, seasoning to taste. Beat the eggs well with ½ teaspoon salt and ⅛ teaspoon pepper. Heat the oil in a small skillet, brushing it over the bottom and sides. Pour in the eggs and cook until almost set. Spoon the meat mixture over half the omelet and flip or fold over the other half. Sprinkle with bacon pieces and serve from the skillet. Makes 2 servings.

---

## Basic Crêpes

---

*Crêpes are glamorous to serve, delectable to eat, and not half as difficult to prepare as most of us have been led to believe. Special crêpe pans are available, but crêpes can also be easily made in a skillet.*

2 eggs
1 cup flour
¼ teaspoon salt
1 cup cold milk
3 tablespoons butter

Beat the eggs with the flour and salt until smooth, then gradually add the milk, beating constantly, until the batter is smooth. (Or combine and mix in a blender or food processor.) Refrigerate the batter, covered, for at least 30 minutes or for up to 24 hours. Heat the butter in an 8-inch crêpe pan or skillet over medium heat. Pour in 3 tablespoons batter, tilting and rotating the pan so that the batter coats the bottom. Cook for about 2 minutes, or until set; flip over and brown the other side. Remove to a plate or clean towel. Makes about 8–10 crêpes. Note: These can be frozen for future use.

# Meat-Filled Crêpes

1 pound ground beef
Butter
½ cup minced onion
½ cup chopped stuffed olives
Salt and pepper
10 Crêpes (p. 74)
1 cup Cheese Sauce (p. 278), heated
½ cup slivered almonds, sautéed

Brown the beef in a skillet, stirring with a fork, until all the red color is gone. Pour off excess fat and transfer the meat to a bowl. Add 1 tablespoon butter to the skillet and sauté the onion over moderate heat until soft; add it to the beef. Add the olives and season to taste with salt and pepper; cool. Fill each crêpe with a spoonful of the meat mixture and roll it up. Place the crêpes, seam side down, on an oven-proof serving platter. Top with Cheese Sauce and almonds and bake in a preheated 400° F. oven until the sauce is brown and bubbly. Makes 5 or more servings.

# Ricotta Crêpes with Meat-Mushroom Sauce

1 pound ricotta cheese
¼ pound Muenster cheese
¼ teaspoon nutmeg
Salt
Pepper
10 Crêpes (p. 74)
2 tablespoons butter
2 tablespoons freshly grated Parmesan cheese
3 cups Meat-Mushroom Sauce (p. 266), heated

Stir together the ricotta, Muenster, nutmeg and a dash of salt and pepper. Divide this mixture among each crêpe. Fold in the 2 sides of each and arrange the filled crêpes in a single layer in a shallow buttered baking dish. Dot with the butter and sprinkle with Parmesan. Bake in a preheated 350° F. oven for 12–15 minutes, or until bubbling hot. Place 2 crêpes on each plate and top with the sauce. Makes 5 servings.

# Meat and Cheese Soufflé

Butter
2 tablespoons freshly grated Parmesan cheese
½ pound ground beef
2 tablespoons minced onion
4 tablespoons flour
2 cups milk
½ cup grated Cheddar cheese
½ cup minced celery
½ cup chopped mushrooms
1 teaspoon Dijon mustard
1 teaspoon curry powder
Salt and pepper
4 egg yolks, beaten
5 egg whites

Butter a 2-quart soufflé dish and sprinkle with Parmesan cheese until the sides and bottom are evenly coated. Cook the beef and onion in a little butter in a small skillet, stirring, until the meat loses its red color. Pour off any excess fat and set aside. Heat 4 tablespoons butter in a saucepan. Stir in the flour and cook for a few minutes over low heat. Add the milk and stir rapidly with a wire whisk until the mixture is thick and smooth. Add the cheese and continue stirring until the cheese melts. Add the cooked meat, the celery, mushrooms and seasonings and stir until the mixture bubbles. Remove from the heat and gradually stir in the egg yolks. Cool to lukewarm. In a large bowl beat the egg whites until stiff. Gently fold the meat mixture into egg whites. Pour this mixture into a soufflé dish and bake for 40 minutes in a preheated 350° F. oven. Makes 6 servings.

# Gnocchi Casserole

*Pronounced* n-YAWK-ee, *this delicate Italian creation is usually shaped into dumplings, covered with sauce and baked. In this American version, gnocchi is treated more like cornmeal mush, but it remains light and delicious.*

10 tablespoons uncooked farina
2 medium onions, chopped very fine
1 tablespoon oil
2 cups grated Swiss or mild Cheddar cheese
½ teaspoon salt
1 tablespoon butter, melted
1 pound ground beef
2 cups Tomato Sauce (p. 263)
½ cup sliced black olives
½ cup freshly grated Parmesan cheese

Boil 3 cups water in the top of a double boiler. Boil more water in the bottom of the double boiler on another burner. When the top water is ready, stir in the farina. Simmer, stirring, for a minute or two, then place the pot over the boiling water in the bottom pot. At the same time, sauté the onion in the oil until it is transparent. Stir 1 cup of the grated Swiss or Cheddar into the farina. Add all but 2 tablespoons of the sautéed onions and add the salt. Butter a shallow baking dish and smooth the farina into it, brushing the top with the melted butter to keep a skin from forming. Refrigerate to cool. Sauté the beef, breaking it up with a fork, until it loses its red color; drain off any excess fat. Add the Tomato Sauce and olives. Spread this meat mixture over the farina and top with the remaining Swiss or Cheddar cheese, the Parmesan cheese and the remaining onions. Bake in a preheated 350° F. oven for 25 minutes. If you decide to refrigerate the dish until you are ready to bake and serve it, bake for about 50 minutes, or until it is golden brown. Makes 6–8 servings.

# Bean, Beef and Sausage Casserole

**2 cans (20 ounces each) cannellini (white kidney beans),**
 **undrained**
**½ pound pork sausage**
**1 onion, chopped**
**2 cloves garlic, crushed**
**1 pound ground beef**
**1 teaspoon salt**
**¼ teaspoon pepper**
**1 tablespoon parsley**
**1 cup white cooking wine**
**1 cup Tomato Sauce (p. 263)**
**½ teaspoon thyme**
**¼ teaspoon basil**

Drain the beans and reserve 1 cup of the liquid. Brown the sausage in a skillet. Add the onion and garlic and sauté until lightly browned. Pour off excess fat, add the beef and sauté until browned. Drain off fat. Add the salt, pepper and parsley. In 3-quart casserole alternate layers of the beans with meat mixture, beginning with the beans. In a saucepan combine the wine, Tomato Sauce, thyme, basil and the reserved bean liquid and bring to a boil. Pour this over the ingredients in the casserole and bake in a preheated 350° F. oven for about 1 hour. Makes 6–8 servings.

## Ground Beef and
## Kidney Bean Skillet

1 pound ground beef
1 clove garlic, halved
1 onion, quartered and sliced
1 can (16 ounces) red kidney beans
1 tablespoon or more chili powder
1 teaspoon salt
1 cup shredded Cheddar cheese

In a large skillet, brown the beef and garlic lightly, stirring it with a fork to break up the meat; drain off the excess fat and discard the garlic. Add the onion and cook, stirring, for about 5 minutes, or until the onion is golden. Add the beans, chili powder and salt, cover and simmer for 15 minutes. Sprinkle with cheese, cover and cook over low heat for 5 minutes, or until the cheese is melted. Makes 4 servings.

## Texas Bean Bake

2 tablespoons oil
½ pound ground beef
1½ cups diced onion
½ cup diced green pepper
¼ cup diced celery
1 package (1¼ ounces) chili seasoning mix
1 cup Tomato Sauce (p. 263)
1 can (20 ounces) red kidney beans, drained

Heat the oil in a skillet and, breaking up the meat with a fork as it cooks, sauté the beef, onion, green pepper and celery until the vegetables are crisp-tender. Stir in the seasoning mix, Tomato Sauce and beans. Bake in a 1½-quart casserole in a preheated 350° F. oven for 30 minutes, or until everything is hot and bubbly. Makes 4 servings.

# Chili con Carne

*Chili powder is one of the top ten spices sold. Blends vary, but the basic ingredients are cayenne pepper, chili pepper, cumin seeds, oregano and garlic powder. Chili dishes are even tastier when served with corn bread, crackers or rice.*

¾ teaspoon minced garlic
1 tablespoon oil
2 pounds ground beef
2 tablespoons chili powder
2½ teaspoons salt
1½ teaspoons cumin seeds
2 cans (16 ounces each) tomatoes, undrained
¼ cup tomato paste
½ teaspoon sugar
1 can (16 ounces) kidney beans, drained

Soften the garlic in 1 teaspoon water. Put it, undrained, in a pot with the oil. Sauté it for 1–2 minutes. Then add the meat and cook, stirring, until the beef loses its red color. Drain off excess fat. Stir in the chili powder, salt, cumin and tomatoes. Bring to a boil and simmer, uncovered, for 25 minutes. Add tomato paste and sugar and simmer for 15 minutes. Add the beans and heat. Makes 6 servings.

# Hot Chili con Carne

1 pound dried red, pink or pinto beans
⅓ cup chopped beef suet
2 onions, chopped
1 clove garlic, minced
2 pounds ground beef
3 teaspoons salt
¼ teaspoon pepper
1–3 teaspoons chili powder
¼ teaspoon crushed red pepper
1 teaspoon paprika
4 cups tomato juice

Put the beans in a kettle or Dutch oven. Add 6 cups water, bring to a boil and boil for 2 minutes. Cover and let stand for 1 hour. Then bring to a boil again, cover and simmer for 2 hours, or until tender. Drain. In a large skillet, render the beef suet. Add the onions and garlic and cook until golden brown. Add the meat and cook, breaking it up with a fork, until the meat loses its red color and browns slightly. Drain off the excess fat. Add the meat, along with the remaining ingredients, to the beans. Simmer, uncovered, stirring occasionally, for about 1½ hours. Makes 8 servings.

# Chili con Carne
# without Tomatoes

*As any Texan will tell you, there are an infinite number of chili dishes. Some, like this one, don't even have tomatoes in them.*

2 pounds ground beef
2 tablespoons chili powder
2 tablespoons minced onion
1 tablespoon paprika
1 tablespoon salt
1 teaspoon minced garlic
1 teaspoon cumin
1 teaspoon sugar
½ teaspoon oregano
¼ teaspoon cayenne
1 tablespoon Worcestershire sauce
3 tablespoons flour

Sauté the beef in a skillet, stirring to break up the meat. Drain off excess fat. Add 3 cups water, bring to a boil, cover and simmer for 30 minutes. Add the remaining ingredients, except the flour, and simmer, covered, for 15 minutes. Blend the flour with ¼ cup water and stir this mixture into the ingredients in the skillet. Cook, stirring, until everything is slightly thickened. Makes 6 servings.

## Three-Meat Chili con Carne

1½ pounds ground beef
¾ pound ground pork
¾ pound ground veal
2 cups chopped onion
1 tablespoon each salt and turmeric
2 tablespoons coriander
3 tablespoons chili powder
1½ teaspoons chopped hot green pepper (fresh or
   canned)
2 cans (16 ounces each) tomatoes, undrained
2 cans (16 ounces each) red kidney beans, drained

In a kettle or Dutch oven combine the meats with the onion, seasonings and hot green pepper. Cook, stirring to break up the meat, for 15 minutes. Drain off the excess fat. Add the tomatoes and simmer, covered, for 20 minutes. Add the beans and simmer for about 10 minutes longer. Makes about 3 quarts, or 8–10 servings.

# Chili-Cornmeal Roundup

1 pound ground beef
1 medium onion, chopped
1 green pepper, chopped
2 cans (16 ounces each) tomatoes, undrained
1 can (12 ounces) tomato paste
2 teaspoons chili powder
1½ teaspoons salt
1½ teaspoons coriander
1 teaspoon cumin
½ teaspoon thyme, crumbled
½ teaspoon oregano, crumbled
2 teaspoons red wine vinegar
½ ounce unsweetened chocolate
1 clove garlic, minced or mashed
1 can (16 ounces) red kidney beans, drained
Cornmeal Ring (see next page)
¾ pound sharp Cheddar cheese, shredded (about 3 cups)
¾ cup very finely sliced scallions (green onion) with
    part of green tops
About ½ head iceberg lettuce, shredded fine
1 ripe avocado, peeled and sliced or diced

In a large casserole or Dutch oven, cook the beef, stirring frequently, over medium heat until crumbly. Drain off excess fat. Add the onion and pepper and sauté until the onion is limp. Stir in the tomatoes, tomato paste, seasonings, vinegar, chocolate, garlic and 1½ cups water. Bring to a boil and simmer, uncovered, stirring occasionally, for 1¾ hours. Add the beans and simmer for 15 minutes longer. At serving time turn the chili into the center of the baked Cornmeal Ring and sprinkle with the cheese and onions. Surround with the lettuce and garnish with avocado slices. Makes 6–8 servings.

CORNMEAL RING

1¼ cups yellow cornmeal
1½ teaspoons salt
2½ cups cold water
5 tablespoons butter, melted

Stir the cornmeal and salt together. In a large saucepan heat the 2½ cups water to boiling; add the cornmeal mixture. Cook, stirring, until the mixture comes to a full boil. Then cook over medium heat, whisking, for 5 minutes. Allow to cook, stirring occasionally, until the mixture will hold its shape when dropped from a spoon. With a tablespoon dipped in cold water, spoon out ovals (about 3 by 1½ by 1½ inches each) of cornmeal mixture close together onto a buttered shallow bake-proof serving platter, forming a ring. (Or spoon the mixture onto a greased baking sheet and transfer it to a serving plate after baking.) Using a brush, coat the ring at once with the melted butter. Bake in a preheated 400° F. oven for 20 minutes.

# Chili con Carne for a Crowd

*Perfect for an informal Friday night party.*

4 pounds ground beef
2 pounds ground pork
6 cups chopped onion
¼ cup diced celery
4 cans (16 ounces each) tomatoes, undrained
2 cans (16 ounces each) tomato puree
8 cans (16 ounces each) red kidney beans, undrained
3 tablespoons salt
½ cup chili powder
Crackers (optional)

Put the meats into shallow broiler-proof pans and brown under broiler. Pour off the drippings into a heavy kettle. Add the onion and celery to the drippings and cook for 5 minutes. Add the meat and the remaining ingredients and simmer, uncovered, over low heat, stirring frequently for about 2 hours. Serve in bowls, with crackers if desired. Makes 25 servings, 2 cups each.

Note: If preferred, omit the pork and use 6 pounds ground beef.

# Texas Hash

1 pound ground beef
1 cup chopped onion
¾ cup chopped green pepper
1 clove garlic
1 can (16 ounces) tomatoes, undrained
¾ cup water
⅓ cup uncooked rice
1½ teaspoons chili powder
1¼ teaspoons salt
¼ teaspoon pepper

Breaking up the meat with a fork as it cooks, sauté the beef, onion, green pepper and garlic until the onion is tender. Drain off excess fat. Add the remaining ingredients and bring to a boil. Reduce heat, cover and simmer for 15 minutes, or until the rice is tender. Makes 4 servings.

# Ground Beef Skillet

1½ pounds ground beef
1 onion, chopped
½ cup chopped green pepper
2 cups Tomato Sauce (p. 263)
1 teaspoon each salt and oregano
½ teaspoon basil
¼ teaspoon pepper
1 cup shredded or diced mozzarella cheese

In a large skillet brown the beef lightly, breaking it up with a fork as it cooks; drain off excess fat. Stir in the onion and green pepper and cook, stirring occasionally, for about 5 minutes, or until tender. Stir in the Tomato Sauce, salt, oregano, basil and pepper; cover and simmer over low heat for 10 minutes. Sprinkle with cheese, cover and simmer for about 5 minutes longer, or until the cheese is melted. Makes 4–6 servings.

# Hamburger and
# Hot Dog Casserole

*It doesn't always have to be hot dogs or hamburgers. Once in a while it's fun to have both in one dish.*

1½ pounds ground beef
½ cup chopped onion
1 cup soft bread crumbs
1 egg, slightly beaten
1 tablespoon Dijon mustard
1½ teaspoons salt
¼ teaspoon pepper
1 pound all-beef frankfurters
1 hard-cooked egg, chopped (optional)
2 tablespoons chopped parsley (optional)
Catsup and pickle relish

Mix the beef thoroughly with the onion, bread crumbs, egg, mustard, salt and pepper. Spread half of the mixture evenly in a shallow baking dish. Cut the frankfurters in half lengthwise and lay half of them on the hamburger so that they look like the spokes of a wheel, all meeting at the center. You may have to trim the frankfurters. Cover with the remaining hamburger, and repeat the wheel pattern. Cover with a piece of aluminum foil and bake in a preheated 350° F. oven for 1 hour. Sprinkle the top with chopped egg and parsley. Serve with catsup and pickle relish. Makes 8 servings.

# HAMBURGERS and HAMBURGER SANDWICHES

THE HAMBURGERS in this chapter range from the very unpretentious to those fit for elegant luncheon company. Some seem best when wedged inside buns, others make attractive open-faced sandwiches or are good simply eaten with a fork and knife—the decision is ultimately your own. One important word of advice, however: never serve hamburgers on cold buns or on a cold piece of bread— nothing does more damage to the wonderful hamburger taste.

Be sure to check under Main Dishes and Casseroles (pp. 17–90) for a selection of hamburger recipes specifically intended for dinner.

One pound of ground meat may be formed into three or four hamburger patties. Ground beef is perishable; don't keep it in your refrigerator for more than one or two days. Use leftover meat in casseroles or with pasta and rice. Leftover cooked meat can also be substituted for fresh meat in many of these recipes.

Some people prefer crusty hamburgers to evenly browned ones. They're easy to make that way in a frying pan if you don't mind the splatter and mess. Simply turn the heat up as high as possible under the pan and brown the hamburger very quickly in its own fat, pressing down on it as it cooks. (If the meat is very lean, you may need to use a small amount of fat.) You'll get a burger as good as any cooked on an outdoor grill.

When charcoal-broiling hamburgers, remember that the timing will vary, depending on how hot the coals are. Always allow at least five minutes on each side for a rare hamburger.

When freezing ground beef, use tightly tied polyethylene bags with all the air pressed out of them, or form the meat into patties and wrap and freeze them individually in foil or plastic wrap. Label the packages to indicate when the meat was frozen. It will keep for two to three months in your freezer.

# Panfried (or "Panbroiled") Hamburgers

*Meat with a large fat content may require less oil or no oil at all. This is especially true when using pans with nonstick linings.*

**2 pounds ground beef**
**Salt and freshly ground black pepper**
**Butter or oil ( or half butter and half oil )**

Form the meat into 6 patties, handling them as little as possible and seasoning to taste with salt and pepper. Heat the butter or oil in a skillet; the pan should be covered with a very thin coating. When the pan is hot (but *not* smoking), cook the patties over medium-high heat for 4 minutes per side, or until well browned. Reduce the heat slightly and cook for 2–4 minutes longer on each side. Makes 6 servings.

# Broiled Hamburgers

2 pounds ground beef
⅔ cup ice water
Salt and freshly ground black pepper
Melted butter

Mix the beef and water lightly but thoroughly, seasoning to taste with the salt and pepper. Form into 6 patties, each about 1 inch thick. Place on a greased broiler rack and brush with melted butter. Broil in a preheated broiler 3–4 inches from the heat for 3–7 minutes. Turn the patties over, brush with more butter, and broil them for 3–7 minutes longer. The total cooking time should be: 6 minutes for rare, 10 minutes for medium, and 14 minutes for well-done hamburgers. Makes 6 servings.

# A Dozen Hamburger Relishes

We tend to think of hamburger relish as the green or red stuff bought in jars. But there are many other kinds of relish, and it's possible also to invent your own. Here are twelve suggestions that may inspire you to proceed on your own.

1. Mix ½ cup chili sauce and 3 tablespoons horse-radish.
2. Add 2 teaspoons sugar and 1 tablespoon vinegar to 1 cup fried onions.

3. Mix ½ cup prepared mustard and 2 chopped dill pickles.

4. Season 1 diced cucumber with 2 teaspoons mustard seeds and 1 chopped onion.

5. Add crumbled crisp bacon to Russian dressing.

6. Mix 1 cup sour cream, 2 tablespoons chopped scallion (green onion) tops and 1 tablespoon chopped fresh dill.

7. Mix 1 cup sliced scallions (green onion), a few caraway seeds and 2 tablespoons vinegar. Season to taste.

8. Peel and dice 1 cucumber. Sprinkle with ½ teaspoon salt and 1 tablespoon sugar. Add 2 tablespoons each red wine vinegar and chopped fresh mint.

9. Mix ¾ cup mayonnaise, ½ cup prepared mustard and 2 tablespoons horseradish. Top with sliced dill pickles.

10. Season butter with chili powder.

11. Mix shredded Cheddar cheese with hot dog or hamburger relish.

12. Chop up pickled beets.

## Delectable Hamburgers

2 tablespoons minced onion
1 tablespoon heavy cream
Freshly ground black pepper
2 pounds ground beef
1 tablespoon butter
1 tablespoon oil
Salt
6 English muffins, split and toasted

Add the onion, cream and pepper to the meat and mix lightly. Shape into 6 patties, each about 1 inch thick. Heat the butter and oil in a heavy skillet. Add patties and cook over medium-high heat, 4–5 minutes on each side, following directions for Panfried Hamburgers (p. 95). Add salt to taste. Serve on English muffins. Makes 6 servings.

## Broiled Beef Patties with Herb Butter

1½ pounds ground beef
6 tablespoons butter, softened
2 tablespoons minced parsley
2 tablespoons minced scallion (green onion) tops or chives
½–¾ teaspoon minced rosemary or one of the following:
   marjoram, basil, savory, dill or thyme

Shape the beef into 4 or 5 patties and broil, following directions for Broiled Hamburgers (p. 96). Mix the butter, parsley, scallion tops and herbs of your choice. Spread on top of the patties before serving. Makes 4–5 servings.

# Hamburgers aux Fines Herbes

2 pounds ground beef
1 tablespoon chopped chives
¾ teaspoon tarragon, crumbled
2 teaspoons salt
¼ teaspoon pepper
¼ cup each chopped parsley and scallions (green onion)
1 egg
Butter, softened

Lightly mix all ingredients except the butter. Shape into 6 patties, handling them as little as possible. Brush with butter and broil (see p. 96) to desired doneness. Makes 6 servings.

# Cumin Hamburgers

*Cumin is one of the world's oldest spices, originating in Egypt. It has been used as a flavoring and as a medicine for thousands and thousands of years. Today it is commonly used as an essential ingredient of curry and chili powders.*

1½ pounds ground beef
1 tablespoon minced onion
1½ teaspoons salt
¾ teaspoon cumin
¼ teaspoon pepper
⅛ teaspoon garlic powder

Combine all ingredients and mix together lightly. Shape into 6 patties, each about ½ inch think and panfry (p. 95) to desired doneness. Makes 6 servings.

## Mushroom-Basil Burgers

¼ pound mushrooms, chopped
1½ pounds ground beef
¼ cup minced onion
1½ teaspoons salt
1 teaspoon basil
¼ teaspoon pepper

Lightly mix all the ingredients together. Shape into 6 patties and broil (see p. 96) to desired doneness. Makes 6 servings.

## Open-faced Hamburgers au Poivre

1 pound ground beef
2 teaspoons cracked or freshly ground black pepper
1 tablespoon butter
2 tablespoons brandy
4 thick slices French bread, toasted
⅓ cup heavy cream
1–2 teaspoons soy sauce
Chopped parsley

Lightly shape the beef into 4 patties. Press ¼ teaspoon pepper on each side. Fry the patties in butter over fairly high heat for 2–3 minutes on each side, or to desired doneness. Pour off excess fat. Add the brandy to the hot skillet and ignite for about 30 seconds; cover with the lid to extinguish. Place the patties on the bread. Add cream and soy sauce to the pan and cook and stir until slightly thickened. Pour this sauce over the patties and garnish with parsley. Makes 4 servings.

# Aberdeen Sausage Sandwiches

*This sausage makes delicious sandwiches, but it can also be served as an appetizer or hors d'oeuvre. Just slice it thin and serve on party-size slices of thin rye bread with mustard, mayonnaise and horseradish.*

1 pound ground beef
½ pound ground smoked ham
1 cup soft bread crumbs
2 tablespoons Worcestershire sauce
2 teaspoons grated lemon rind
1 teaspoon sugar
1 teaspoon salt
2 eggs
Flour

Mix all the ingredients except the flour. Shape the mixture into a roll about 2½ inches in diameter. Roll this in flour and wrap it in a double thickness of cheesecloth, tying each end of the cloth with a string. Put it on a rack in a kettle and cover with boiling water. Bring to a boil and simmer for 1½ hours. Cool it in the broth. Chill and slice thin. Serve on rye bread with mustard, mayonnaise and horseradish. Makes 4 sandwich servings, or 12–16 appetizer servings.

## Hamburgers Deluxe

*Serve on toasted buns, as open-faced sandwiches or with no bread at all.*

2 tablespoons butter
2 ribs celery, in ½-inch diagonal slices
1 medium onion, chopped
¼ pound mushrooms, sliced thin
2 pounds ground beef
Salt and pepper
Freshly grated Parmesan cheese

Melt the butter in a skillet and sauté the celery, onion and mushrooms for about 5 minutes, or until the celery is crisp-tender; set aside. Meanwhile shape the beef into 6 patties. With your fingers indent the center of each patty, crimping the edge to form a ridge. Broil on a broiler rack (see p. 96) to desired doneness. Season with salt and pepper. Fill the centers with the sautéed vegetables, sprinkle with Parmesan and broil a few minutes more until golden. Makes 6 servings.

# Bacon-Cheese Hamburgers

2 pounds ground beef
6 strips bacon, partially cooked
Crushed rosemary
Coarsely ground black pepper
6 slices Cheddar or Swiss cheese

Shape the beef into 6 patties. Wrap a partially cooked bacon strip around each and secure with a toothpick. Season with the rosemary and pepper. Panfry (see p. 95) or broil (see p. 96). Just before the patties are done, top each with a slice of cheese. If broiling, cover them with a piece of foil (if panfrying, cover with the lid), until the cheese is slightly melted.

# Hamburgers with Mustard Sauce

1½ pounds ground beef
2 tablespoons chopped parsley
1¼ teaspoons salt
Dash of pepper
1 medium onion, minced
1 tablespoon butter
2 tablespoons water
2 tablespoons prepared mustard
1 tablespoon Worcestershire sauce
4 English muffins, split and toasted

Mix the beef, parsley, salt, pepper and onion and shape into 4 patties, handling as little as possible. Panfry in the butter in a skillet to desired doneness (see p. 95). Remove to a hot platter. Put the water, mustard and Worcestershire sauce in the skillet and heat, scraping up the brown bits. Put the patties on the English muffin bottoms and pour the sauce over them. Put on muffin tops and serve. Makes 4 servings.

## Hamburger Pil-Pil

1 pound ground beef
1½ teaspoons salt
¼ teaspoon paprika
2 tablespoons tomato juice
1 bunch parsley
1 clove garlic
2 tablespoons white wine
¼ cup almonds, blanched
1 tablespoon oil
½ teaspoon pepper
4 hamburger buns, split
2 tablespoons butter, softened

Mix the beef, 1 teaspoon of the salt and the paprika. Shape into 4 patties and set aside. In a mortar with pestle, pound the remaining salt and the other ingredients, except for the last 2, until fairly fine. Put this mixture in a small skillet and sauté for 2–3 minutes. Cook the hamburger patties as desired (see pp. 95, 96). Spread the buns with the butter, then toast them in the broiler. Place the hamburgers on the buns and serve with the sauce. Makes 4 servings.

# Burgundy Hamburgers

2 pounds ground beef
1½ teaspoons salt
½ cup Burgundy
Freshly ground pepper
2 tablespoons each minced parsley and chives
6 hamburger buns, split, toasted and buttered

Mix lightly but thoroughly the beef, salt, wine, pepper, parsley and chives. Form into 6 patties and broil to desired doneness (see p. 96). Serve on toasted, buttered buns. Makes 6 servings.

# Double-Decker Burgers

1 pound ground beef
¼ cup Russian dressing (see next page)
4 hamburger buns, split and toasted
Pickle slices
¼ cup chopped onion
1 cup shredded lettuce
4 slices American cheese

Divide the beef into 8 portions and shape these into thin patties. Broil to desired doneness (p. 96), turning once. Spoon Russian dressing on the bun bottoms, top each with a patty, pickle, onion, lettuce, a second patty, cheese and a bun top. Makes 4 servings.

RUSSIAN DRESSING

3 tablespoons mayonnaise
1 tablespoon chili sauce

Mix until thoroughly blended.

# Reuben-Style Hamburgers

1 pound ground beef
Prepared mustard
1 cup drained sauerkraut
4 slices Swiss cheese
8 slices rye bread, toasted

Shape the beef into 4 oval patties, each about ¼ inch thick.
Spread with mustard and broil for 3 minutes, or to desired
doneness (see p. 96). Spread a layer of sauerkraut on each
patty, top with a slice of cheese and continue to broil until
melted. Serve between slices of toast. Makes 4 servings.

# The Health Burger

*The growing interest in organic and health foods is re-
flected in contemporary cooking. Some of the new health
food recipes are a little too "healthy tasting" for our liking,
but some, like this one, are a delight.*

2 pounds ground round or sirloin steak
1 medium onion, chopped fine
1 small tomato, peeled and chopped
¼ cup chopped mushrooms
1 cup shredded extra-sharp Cheddar cheese
3 tablespoons wheat germ
2 eggs, slightly beaten
½ teaspoon each salt and pepper
Safflower oil or margarine
Whole wheat or rye toast

Mix all the ingredients except the oil and toast, handling the meat as little as possible. Form into 6 patties. In a skillet heat a small amount of the oil or margarine (just enough to coat the pan) and panfry the hamburgers to desired doneness (see p. 95). Serve on whole wheat or rye toast. Makes 6 servings.

# Piquant Hamburgers

1 pound ground beef
¼ teaspoon salt
⅛ teaspoon pepper
½ teaspoon marjoram, crushed
2 scallions (green onion), sliced thin
2 tablespoons chopped parsley
1 teaspoon garden relish
2 tablespoons capers, drained
¼ cup red cooking wine
1 tablespoon oil (optional)

Thoroughly mix the meat, salt, pepper, marjoram, scallions, parsley, relish, capers and wine. Shape into 4 patties, each about 1 inch thick. Broil (see p. 96) or panfry (see p. 95). Makes 4 servings.

## Tomato Burgers on Parmesan Buns

1 pound ground beef
2 tablespoons chopped onion
2 tablespoons chopped green pepper
4 thick slices tomato
Garlic salt
Pepper
Butter
4 hamburger buns, split
2 tablespoons freshly grated Parmesan cheese

Combine the beef, onion and green pepper. Shape into 4 patties and broil to desired doneness (see p. 96). Top each patty with a tomato slice, sprinkle with garlic salt and pepper and dot with butter. Broil close to the heat until sizzling. Spread bun halves with butter, sprinkle with Parmesan and toast them under the broiler. Serve the patties on these buns. Makes 4 servings.

# Cheesy Walnut Burgers

1 pound ground beef
1 tablespoon red table wine
2 teaspoons Worcestershire sauce
1 teaspoon Dijon mustard
½ teaspoon salt
½ teaspoon pepper
½ cup shredded Cheddar cheese
½ cup chopped walnuts

Lightly mix the beef, wine, Worcestershire sauce, mustard, and salt and pepper. Add the cheese and nuts, handling the meat as little as possible. Shape the meat into 4 patties. Broil to desired doneness (see p. 96). Makes 4 servings.

# Bacon-Nut Burgers

6 strips bacon
1½ pounds ground beef
1½ teaspoons salt
⅛ teaspoon pepper
6 tablespoons chopped nuts
3 tablespoons chopped parsley
2 tablespoons grated onion

Cook the bacon until crisp; drain. Mix the beef, salt and pepper; divide this into 12 equal portions and roll them with a rolling pin between 2 sheets of waxed paper to form thin patties, each about 5 inches in diameter. Mix the last

3 ingredients together and spread this on 6 of the patties. Top each with a bacon strip. Cover with remaining 6 patties and pinch the edges together. Broil to desired doneness (see p. 96), turning once. Makes 6 servings.

# Walnut Surprise Burgers

¾ cup finely chopped walnuts
1 teaspoon dillseed
Red wine
Salt
1 pound ground beef

Mix all the ingredients together, handling the meat as little as possible. Shape into 3 or 4 patties and cook in your favorite manner. Makes 3–4 servings.

# Pecan Hamburgers in Wine

1½ pounds ground beef
1 teaspoon salt
½ teaspoon pepper
¾ cup coarsely chopped pecans
½ cup red table wine

Mix well the beef, salt, pepper and pecans, handling as little as possible. Shape into 10–12 thin patties. Brown on both sides in a heavy skillet. Add the wine, cover and simmer for 5 minutes, or to desired doneness. Makes 5–6 servings.

# Apple and Almond Surprise Burgers

½ cup peeled and grated tart apple
1 scallion (green onion), minced
⅓ cup chopped almonds, toasted
Red wine
1 pound ground beef

Mix all of the ingredients together, handling the meat as little as possible. Shape into 3 or 4 patties and cook in your favorite manner. Makes 3–4 servings.

# Cheddar Surprise Burgers

1 cup shredded Cheddar cheese
1 clove garlic, minced
White wine
Salt and pepper
1 pound ground beef

Mix all the ingredients together, handling the meat as little as possible. Shape into 3 or 4 patties and cook in your favorite manner. Makes 3–4 servings.

# Mushroom and Relish Surprise Burgers

¾ cup finely chopped mushrooms
3 pinches of marjoram
Dollop of piccalilli
White wine
Salt and pepper
1 pound ground beef

Mix well all the ingredients, handling the meat as little as possible. Shape into 3 or 4 patties and cook in your favorite manner. Makes 3–4 servings.

# Red, Green and Blue Burgers

⅓ cup crumbled blue cheese
¼ cup minced radishes
2 tablespoons minced scallions (green onion)
2 tablespoons light cream
1 pound ground beef

Cream the cheese. Add the radishes, scallions and light cream and mix well. Flatten the beef into a 12-by-6-inch rectangle and, with a wet knife, cut it into 8 equal squares. Spread the cheese mixture on top of 4 of the patties, leaving ¾ inch clear around the edges. Top with the remaining squares. With hands dipped in cold water, crimp the edges of the hamburgers so that the filling is tucked completely inside. Broil 5–6 inches from the heat to desired doneness (see p. 96). Makes 4 servings.

# California Sandwichburgers

1 pound ground beef
4 slices avocado, each ¼ inch thick
Salt and coarsely ground black pepper
4 strips bacon, cooked crisp

Flatten the beef into a 12-by-6-inch rectangle and, with a wet knife, cut it into 8 equal squares. Place a slice of avocado on each of 4 of the squares. Season to taste with salt and pepper. Cut the bacon slices in half and arrange them in a crisscross pattern on top of the avocado slices. Cover with the remaining hamburger squares. With hands dipped in cold water, crimp the edges of the hamburgers so that the filling is tucked completely inside. Broil 5–6 inches from the heat to desired doneness (see p. 96). Makes 4 servings.

# Mostly Onion Sandwichburgers

2 cups chopped onion
1 tablespoon butter
¾ teaspoon paprika
2 tablespoons sour cream
Salt
1 pound ground beef

Sauté the onion in the butter until browned. Add the paprika, sour cream and salt to taste and mix well. Flatten the beef into a 12-by-6-inch rectangle and, with a wet knife, cut into 8 equal squares. Spread the onion mixture on top of each of 4 of the patties, leaving ¾ inch clear around the edges. Top with the remaining patties. With hands dipped in cold water, crimp edges of the hamburgers so that the filling is tucked completely inside. Broil 5–6 inches from the heat to desired doneness (see p. 96). Makes 4 servings.

## Piquant Beet and Onion Sandwichburgers

¼ cup finely chopped pickled beets
2 tablespoons minced onion
1 tablespoon capers, drained
1 egg yolk
Salt and pepper
1 pound ground beef

Mix the beets, onion, capers and egg yolk and season with salt and pepper to taste. Flatten the beef into a 12-by-6-inch rectangle and, with a wet knife, cut it into 8 equal squares. Place the filling on top of each of 4 of the patties, leaving ¾ inch clear around the edges. Top with the remaining patties. With hands dipped in cold water, crimp the edges of the hamburgers so that the filling is tucked completely inside. Broil 5–6 inches from the heat to desired doneness (see p. 96). Makes 4 servings.

# Italian Sandwichburgers

½ cup freshly grated Parmesan cheese
1 small garlic clove, minced
1 teaspoon basil
2 tablespoons olive oil
¼ cup finely chopped walnuts
1 pound ground beef

Mix well the Parmesan cheese, garlic, basil, olive oil and walnuts. Flatten the beef into a 12-by-6-inch rectangle and, with a wet knife, cut it into 8 equal squares. Spread the Parmesan-walnut mixture on top of each of 4 of the patties, leaving ¾ inch clear around the edges. Top with the remaining patties. With hands dipped in cold water, crimp the edges of the hamburgers so that the filling is tucked completely inside. Broil 5–6 inches from the heat to desired doneness (see p. 96). Makes 4 servings.

# Spanish-Style Hamburgers

1 pound ground beef
¼ cup Tomato Sauce (p. 263)
¼ cup chopped stuffed olives
¼ cup raisins, soaked in water a few minutes
⅓ cup minced onion
⅓ cup chopped green pepper
¼ teaspoon oregano, crushed
¾ teaspoon salt
¼ teaspoon pepper
½ cup canned chick-peas, drained

Thoroughly mix the meat, Tomato Sauce, olives, raisins, onion, green pepper, oregano, salt and pepper. Work in the chick-peas and shape into 4 patties, each about 1 inch thick. Broil (see p. 96) or panfry (see p. 95) to desired doneness. Makes 4 servings.

## Hamburgers with Spanish Hot Sauce

2 medium tomatoes, peeled and chopped fine
1 medium red onion, chopped fine
½ green pepper, chopped fine
½ teaspoon salt
⅛ teaspoon each black pepper and crushed red pepper
1 tablespoon lemon juice
1½ pounds ground beef

Mix all the ingredients except the beef, and let stand in the refrigerator for several hours or longer. Form the beef into 6 patties and cook in your favorite manner. Serve with the cold sauce. Makes 6 servings.

# Tangy Tomato-Sauced Hamburgers

*Leftover sauce will keep in the refrigerator for several days.*

2 tablespoons butter
1 small onion, chopped
1 cup tomato juice
1 tablespoon red wine vinegar
1 tablespoon lemon juice
2 tablespoons dark molasses
½ teaspoon hot pepper sauce
1 teaspoon dry mustard
½ teaspoon salad herbs
1 clove garlic, minced
2 pounds ground beef

Melt the butter in a saucepan. Add the onion and sauté until limp. Add the remaining ingredients except the beef and bring to a boil. Reduce heat and simmer for a few minutes. Meanwhile form the beef into 6–8 patties. Brush the sauce on the hamburgers before grilling or broiling, then cook to desired doneness. Makes 6–8 servings.

## Chili-Honey Glazed Hamburgers

*Wonderful when cooked over a grill.*

¼ cup chili sauce
2 tablespoons lemon juice
2 tablespoons honey
1 teaspoon dry mustard
½ teaspoon salt
¼ teaspoon pepper
1 pound ground beef

In a small saucepan mix all the ingredients except the beef. Heat gently, stirring, for a few minutes. Shape the beef into 4 patties and brush glaze on top of each before grilling or broiling (not panfrying) to desired doneness. Makes 4 servings.

## Hamburgers with Snappy Curried Chili Sauce

1 cup chili sauce
1–2 teaspoons curry powder
1 tablespoon honey
2 pounds ground beef

Mix the chili sauce, curry powder and honey in a small saucepan. Heat gently, stirring, for a few minutes. Shape the beef into 8 patties and brush sauce on top before grilling or broiling to desired doneness. Makes 8 servings.

# Hamburgers with Pepper-Steak Topping

1 cup diced green pepper
1 tablespoon soy sauce
1 tablespoon sherry
½ teaspoon sugar
¼ cup cold water
2 teaspoons cornstarch
1½ pounds ground beef

Mix the green pepper, soy sauce, sherry, sugar and water in a small saucepan. Simmer for about 5 minutes, then stir in the cornstarch mixed with a little cold water. Cook, stirring, until thickened. Meanwhile shape the beef into 6 patties and cook as desired. Serve the sauce hot on top of the cooked hamburgers. Makes 6 servings.

# Hamburgers Topped with Marinated Onions

*The onions should be marinated a day in advance.*

1 large Spanish onion, sliced
¼ teaspoon each salt and pepper
¼ teaspoon either basil, rosemary or sage
3 tablespoons vinegar
2 tablespoons oil
2 pounds ground beef

The night before you plan to serve this dish, prepare the marinated onions by covering the onion slices with boiling water and allowing to stand for about 30 minutes; drain. Put the onion slices in a bowl and sprinkle with the salt, pepper and herb. Mix the vinegar and oil together and pour over the onions. Cover and chill overnight. Shape the beef into 6–8 hamburgers, cook as desired and serve with onions on top. Makes 6–8 servings.

## Hamburgers Smothered with Onions

5 medium onions, sliced
2 tablespoons butter
½ teaspoon sugar
Salt and pepper
1½ pounds ground beef
1 teaspoon seasoned salt
¼ teaspoon seasoned pepper

Sauté the onions in butter in a skillet until golden brown. Add ¾ cup water, the sugar and salt and pepper to taste. Bring to a boil and simmer for 10 minutes. Lightly mix the beef and seasonings and shape into 4 patties. Panfry to desired doneness (see p. 95) and top with onions. Makes 4 servings.

# Hamburgers Topped with Avocado and Tomato

1 avocado
1½ teaspoons lemon juice
1 teaspoon grated onion
¼ teaspoon salt
6 drops hot pepper sauce
1 pound ground beef
4 slices tomato

Peel and mash the avocado. Stir in the lemon juice, onion, salt and hot pepper sauce. Meanwhile shape the beef into 4 patties and broil (see p. 96) or panfry (see p. 95) to desired doneness. Spoon the avocado mixture on top of the hamburgers and top each with a slice of tomato. Makes 4 servings.

# Snappy Sour Cream Hamburgers

1 pound ground beef
½ cup sour cream
1 tablespoon prepared horseradish
½ cup coarsely chopped tart red apple

Form the beef into 4 patties and panfry (see p. 95) or broil (see p. 96) to desired doneness. Meanwhile mix the remaining ingredients. When the hamburgers are ready to be served, cover with the sauce. Makes 4 servings.

## Hamburgers Stroganoff

2 tablespoons chopped onion
3 tablespoons butter
1 pound ground beef
¼ pound mushrooms, sliced
Salt and pepper
½ cup sour cream, at room temperature
Chopped parsley (optional)
2 split hamburger buns or 4 slices bread, buttered and
    toasted

Sauté the onion in 1 tablespoon butter until golden; add
to the beef. Sauté the mushrooms in 2 tablespoons butter
until brown; set aside. Shape the beef mixture into 4 patties
and broil (see p. 96) to desired doneness. Season with
salt and pepper and top with sour cream, mushrooms and
a sprinkling of parsley. Serve on bun halves or bread.
Makes 4 servings.

# Hamburger Capers

¼ cup butter, softened
1 small clove garlic, minced
1 tablespoon chopped parsley
1 loaf French bread, halved lengthwise
1½ pounds ground beef
¼ cup dry red wine
2 tablespoons capers, drained
1 teaspoon salt
¼ teaspoon pepper
2 tomatoes, sliced
1 small green pepper, slivered
1 onion, sliced thin

Combine the butter, garlic and parsley and spread on the bread. Wrap in foil and heat. Combine the beef, wine, capers, salt and pepper. On a broiler pan shape the meat into a loaf slightly longer than the bread. Broil the meat on both sides to desired doneness. Put the meat on one half of the bread and top with tomatoes, green pepper, onion and the other half of the bread. Slice diagonally in sections. Makes 6 servings.

## Hamburger Romesco

¼ cup blanched filberts or almonds
3 fresh sweet red peppers, roasted and peeled, or 1 jar
   (4 ounces) pimientos, drained
3 tablespoons olive oil
¾ teaspoon salt
1 clove garlic
4 hero rolls, each 6 inches long
1 pound ground beef
2 tablespoons tomato juice
½ teaspoon celery salt
¼ teaspoon cayenne

Put the nuts, peppers, 1 tablespoon of the oil, ¼ teaspoon of the salt and the garlic in a mortar and pound with a pestle until almost smooth. Heat, if desired, or use cold. Split the rolls, brush with the remaining oil and toast in a broiler. Mix the beef with the remaining salt and the other ingredients. Shape into 4 patties and cook as desired. Fill the rolls with the hamburgers and serve with the sauce. Makes 4 servings.

# Hamburger Basquaise

1 clove garlic, minced
3 sprigs of parsely, minced
1 tablespoon olive oil
1½ teaspoons red wine vinegar
1 green pepper, in ¼-inch pieces
1 sweet red pepper, in ¼-inch pieces
4 scallions (green onion) with tops, sliced fine
1 small onion, minced
1 tomato, peeled and diced fine
½ teaspoon cayenne
Salt
1 pound ground beef
3 tablespoons tomato juice
¼ teaspoon pepper
12 strips bacon
4 hero rolls, each 6 inches long
¼ cup butter, melted

Mix the garlic, parsley, olive oil, vinegar, green pepper, red pepper, scallions, onion, tomato, cayenne and salt to taste. Let stand for 2 hours at room temperature. Mix 1 teaspoon salt, the beef, tomato juice and pepper. Shape into 4 oblongs to fit the hero rolls. Wrap each patty in 3 strips of bacon and broil to desired doneness (see p. 96). Split the rolls, brush with butter and toast. Serve the meat on rolls and top with the sauce. Makes 4 servings.

## Meatball Heroes

1 pound ground beef
¼ cup minced onion
¼ cup water
1 teaspoon basil
¾ teaspoon salt
Dash of pepper
2 tablespoons oil
1 large green pepper, sliced
2 cups Tomato Sauce (p. 263)
4 hero rolls, heated and slit

Mix the beef, onion, water, basil, salt and pepper. Shape into 1-inch meatballs and brown in hot oil; remove and set aside. Add the green pepper to the drippings in the skillet and sauté until lightly browned. Drain off excess fat. Add the Tomato Sauce and meatballs; cover and simmer for 15 minutes. Serve on rolls. Makes 4 sandwiches.

# Meatball Heroes with Barbecue Sauce

*It is helpful to have frozen meatballs on hand.*

2 cans (16 ounces each) tomatoes, undrained
2 cups finely chopped onion
4 cloves garlic, minced
1 cup cider vinegar
½ cup molasses
⅓ cup packed brown sugar
Dash of hot pepper sauce
24–30 meatballs
6 hero rolls, each 6 inches long

Whirl the tomatoes, onion and garlic in a blender. Pour into a large saucepan and add, stirring, the vinegar, molasses and brown sugar. Simmer for about 2 hours. Add the meatballs and simmer for 30 minutes longer, or until the meatballs are heated through. Serve on rolls. Makes 6 servings.

# Barbecued Hamburgers

*For other barbecue sauce recipes, see pp. 268–270.*

2 pounds ground beef
2 tablespoons butter
Salt and pepper
½ cup catsup
¼ cup vinegar
1 medium onion, chopped
1 tablespoon prepared mustard
1 tablespoon steak sauce

Shape the meat into 6 oval steaks. Brown in the butter, then sprinkle with salt and pepper. Pour off the excess fat. Mix the remaining ingredients and pour over the meat. Cover and cook gently, basting several times with the sauce, for 8–10 minutes, or to desired doneness. Makes 6 servings.

# Barbecued Beef on Rolls

2 pounds ground beef
2 tablespoons butter
1 medium onion, minced
2 tablespoons vinegar
2 tablespoons packed brown sugar
¼ cup lemon juice
1 bottle ( 14 ounces ) catsup
2 tablespoons Worcestershire sauce
½ teaspoon dry mustard
1 cup chopped celery
Salt and pepper
6 hamburger rolls, split and toasted

Cook the beef, breaking it up with a fork, in the butter in a skillet until the meat loses its red color. Add 1 cup water and the remaining ingredients except the rolls. Simmer, uncovered, stirring occasionally, for 10 minutes, or until the vegetables are soft. Serve on rolls. Makes 6 servings.

# Southwest Chili Dogs

½ pound ground beef
1 large onion, chopped
1 cup Tomato Sauce ( p. 263 )
1 teaspoon chili powder
½ teaspoon salt
½ teaspoon Worcestershire sauce
1 pound frankfurters ( 8–10 ), heated
8–10 frankfurter buns, split and toasted

Brown the beef and ½ cup of the onion, stirring to break up the meat. Stir in the Tomato Sauce, chili powder, salt and Worcestershire sauce. Simmer for 10 minutes. Spoon this mixture over the frankfurters in the buns. Sprinkle with the remaining onion if desired. Makes 4–5 servings.

## Meat-Filled French Bread

½ pound sweet Italian sausage meat
½ pound ground beef
½ cup chopped onion
2 medium-sized loaves of brown-and-serve French bread
1 egg
2 tablespoons Dijon mustard
½ teaspoon salt
½ teaspoon pepper
⅛ teaspoon oregano
¼ cup water
2 tablespoons butter, softened
1 clove garlic, crushed

In a heavy skillet cook the sausage meat, breaking it up with a fork, until it loses some of its red color. Add the beef and onion and cook the beef until lightly browned. Drain off excess fat. Slice the loaves open if necessary and hollow them out. Mix the bread crumbs from the loaves with the egg, mustard, salt, pepper, oregano and water. Add the meat and mix lightly but well. Mix the softened butter and garlic, and butter the insides of the loaves. Spread the meat mixture in the loaves. Bake in a preheated 400° F. oven for 15–20 minutes. Cut into serving sizes. Makes 6 servings.

# Sloppy Joes

¾ pound Italian-style bulk sausage
¾ pound ground beef
¼ teaspoon aniseed (optional)
¾ teaspoon garlic powder
¾ teaspoon salt
¼ teaspoon pepper
4 cups Tomato Sauce (p. 263)
¾ teaspoon basil
6 crusty French rolls
12 slices (1 ounce each) mozzarella cheese
Paprika

Brown the sausage and beef, breaking them up with a fork, in a deep, heavy saucepan. If the sausage is not seasoned with anise, add the aniseed. Drain off excess fat. Add the garlic powder, salt, pepper and Tomato Sauce and bring to a boil. Simmer, uncovered, for about 1½ hours. Add the basil and simmer for 30 minutes longer, then skim off the excess fat. Cut the rolls in half lengthwise. Cover the inside top half of each with 2 slices of mozzarella and sprinkle with paprika. Broil until the cheese melts. Spread the meat mixture on the bottom half of the rolls. Put the sandwiches together and serve hot. Makes 6 servings.

# Ground Beef in Pita

*Pita bread is also known as Syrian, Saharan, Middle East-*
*ern and Near Eastern bread. When these round, flat loaves*
*are cut in half, they form pouches ready to be filled with*
*anything from plain butter to the ground beef concoction*
*below.*

4 pita
2 tablespoons butter
2 tablespoons chopped onion
1 clove garlic, minced
2 tablespoons minced green pepper
1 pound ground beef
1 tablespoon prepared mustard
½ teaspoon oregano
1 teaspoon salt
Freshly ground black pepper
1½ cups peeled, seeded and chopped tomatoes

Heat the bread in a low oven. Heat the butter in a skillet
and sauté the onion, garlic and pepper until just soft; do
not brown. Add the beef, mustard, oregano, salt and a
generous amount of pepper. Cook, stirring, until the meat
is no longer red. At the last minute stir in the chopped
tomatoes and cook briefly. Cut the pitas in half and stuff
the pouches. Makes 4 generous servings.

## Tacos

*You can either thaw frozen tortillas for these, or make your own (see p. 135). Preparing taco shells in either fashion takes time, so prepare them first and keep them warm in a low oven. You can also make your own taco sauce if you like (p. 267).*

1 pound ground beef
1 cup chopped onion
½ cup chopped green pepper
1 clove garlic, minced
1 cup Tomato Sauce (p. 263)
1 tablespoon chili powder
1 teaspoon salt
¼ teaspoon pepper
¼ teaspoon hot pepper sauce
12 taco shells, warmed, or 12 prepared tortillas
   (see p. 135)
Chopped tomatoes
Chopped lettuce
Shredded Cheddar or Jack cheese
Taco sauce, bottled (or see p. 267)
Oil

Sauté the beef, onion, green pepper and garlic until the beef is browned and the onion tender. Spoon off excess fat. Stir in the Tomato Sauce, chili powder, salt, pepper and pepper sauce; cook, uncovered, until thickened, about 20 minutes, stirring occasionally. Spoon the meat mixture into the taco shells and top with some tomato, lettuce and cheese. Sprinkle with taco sauce.

*To make taco shells:* Thaw tortillas if frozen. In a skillet heat about ½ inch oil over medium-high heat. Fold a tortilla in half loosely, forming a U. Hold the top with tongs, dip the fold in hot oil and fry a few seconds until fold holds its shape. Turn and, holding one side with tongs, fry each side until crisp and lightly browned. Drain on paper towels. Repeat with the remaining tortillas.

## Tortilla Cheeseburgers

1 pound ground beef
1 small onion, minced
1 small green pepper, minced
1 cup Tomato Sauce (p. 263)
½ teaspoon crushed red pepper
½ teaspoon salt
1 package (8 ounces) process American cheese slices
8 Flour Tortillas (see next page)

Sauté the beef, onion and green pepper, stirring frequently, until the meat is lightly browned. Drain off excess fat. Add Tomato Sauce, red pepper and salt; cook and stir until the meat absorbs most of the sauce. Place 1 cheese slice on each tortilla; top with the meat mixture. Fold the 2 sides of the tortilla toward the center; then, starting with an unfolded edge, roll it up. Serve immediately. Makes 8 servings.

FLOUR TORTILLAS

**2 cups flour**
**¾ teaspoon salt**
**½ cup butter**
**About ½ cup water**

Mix the flour and salt, then cut in the butter until the mixture resembles fine crumbs. Add water and stir until moistened (if necessary add 1–2 tablespoons more water). Divide the dough into 8 portions and shape in balls. Cover with a damp paper towel and let stand for 15–20 minutes. On a lightly floured surface, roll out each ball into a 9- or 10-inch circle. Stack the circles and cover them with a damp towel. Heat a large skillet or griddle until very hot. *Do not add oil.* Bake the tortillas one at a time until they are blistered and the blisters brown. Turn quickly, lifting at the edges with your fingers, and cook the second side. Slip into an envelope of folded foil and keep warm. (Or cool them wrapped in their foil envelope. To freeze, wrap airtight. Reheat in a skillet to make them pliable before filling.) Makes 8 tortillas.

Note: Keep the tortillas covered, or they will become brittle.

# MEATBALLS

SERVE THEM PIPING HOT for dinner or cold as a party snack, perhaps with a special dip (see p. 143). Easy to freeze, quick to thaw, frozen meatballs can be reheated directly from a frozen state, as long as you make sure that they are heated through before you serve them.

It is always handy to have a few dozen or so tucked away in your freezer. Make two or three batches at a time, and freeze what you don't use.

When preparing meatballs, handle the ingredients as lightly as possible. Overhandled meat will produce tough meatballs. And truth to tell, all meatballs end up slightly irregular anyway; no need to try to form them into perfectly round balls.

Meatballs may be fried in fat in a frying pan or baked in the oven. Oven-baking is easier and very satisfactory, especially when the meatballs are to be served in a sauce. Panfrying is best when you want the meatballs to be crisp.

Serve leftover meatballs, hot or cold, in rolls as sandwiches. You can moisten them with a special sauce (pp. 261–278), with a dip (p. 143), with mayonnaise, relish or another condiment of your choice.

Meatballs should be frozen in moisture-proof containers —pint-size containers are especially handy for this. Leave one-half inch of head room to allow for expansion during freezing, and always label the containers, listing the number of meatballs and the date that they were cooked. They will keep well for up to three months. To reheat, arrange them in a shallow baking dish and bake at 325° F. until heated through.

# Basic Meatballs # 1

¼ cup minced onion
3 tablespoons butter
1½ pounds ground beef
¾ cup fine dry bread crumbs
½ cup beef broth, beer or water
2 eggs
1 teaspoon salt
¼ teaspoon pepper
¼ teaspoon allspice (optional)

In a skillet sauté the onion in 1 tablespoon of the butter until brown but not burned. Mix well with the beef, bread crumbs, broth, eggs, salt, pepper and allspice. Form 1½-inch balls. Heat the remaining 2 tablespoons butter until slightly browned. Brown the meatballs, half at a time, over medium heat, shaking the skillet occasionally to brown them evenly. Return all the meatballs to the skillet; cover and cook over low heat until of desired doneness. Serve hot or cold. Makes 5–6 servings.

# Basic Meatballs # 2

1 pound ground beef
⅛ cup soy sauce
¼ teaspoon pepper
½ cup ice water

Mix all the ingredients lightly but thoroughly with your hands, or a wooden spoon if you like. The mixture will be quite soft. Shape into small, 1-to-1½-inch balls. Place in a single layer on an ungreased shallow baking dish. Bake in a preheated 375° F. oven, turning once or twice, for about 30 minutes, or until brown. Makes 3–4 servings.

# Variations on Basic Meatballs

✿❀✿❀✿❀✿❀✿❀✿❀✿❀✿❀✿❀✿❀✿❀✿❀✿❀✿❀✿❀✿❀✿❀

With a teaspoon of this or a teaspoon of that, plain meatballs are quickly transformed. Try adding one or more of the following to either of the basic meatball recipes:

1. 1 to 2 teaspoons ground ginger
2. 1 to 3 teaspoons chili powder
3. 1 to 3 teaspoons curry powder
4. 1 teaspoon hot pepper sauce
5. 2 cloves garlic, crushed
6. ⅓ cup crumbled cooked bacon
7. ½ cup sautéed mushrooms
8. ½ cup finely chopped blanched almonds
9. ⅓ cup minced scallions (green onion)
10. ½ cup freshly grated Parmesan cheese

# Sherry and Soy Dip

*This dip and the following one (Spiced-Up Mayonnaise Dip) are splendid with warm or cold meatballs for party snacks or appetizers.*

1½ cups sherry
⅔ cup soy sauce
⅓ cup packed light or dark brown sugar
5 tablespoons cornstarch

Mix all the ingredients with ¾ cup water in a saucepan and cook, stirring frequently, over medium heat for 5 minutes, or until the mixture boils and then clears. Serve immediately. Makes 2 cups.

# Spiced-Up Mayonnaise Dip

2 cups mayonnaise
2 tablespoons prepared spicy mustard, soy sauce, steak
    sauce, dill, or curry powder

Mix the mayonnaise with the preferred spice. Chill. Makes 2 cups.

## Party Meatballs

½ cup bottled red French dressing
1 slice dry bread, crumbled
1 pound ground beef
½ pound ground veal
½ pound ground pork
1 medium onion, chopped
1 egg
1 teaspoon salt
½ teaspoon pepper
1 tablespoon lemon juice
2 tablespoons chopped parsley
Butter
3 tablespoons flour
1 can (10½ ounces) condensed beef broth or consommé
1 cup dry red or white wine

Mix the dressing and bread in a large bowl. Mix the meats lightly with your hands. Add the meat to the dressing and add onion, egg, salt, pepper, lemon juice and parsley and mix lightly but thoroughly. Shape into balls about 1½ inches in diameter and brown in butter on all sides in a large skillet. When browned, remove from the skillet. Pour off the excess fat and cool the skillet slightly. Then put the flour in the skillet, slowly add the bouillon and wine and stir until smooth. Cook, stirring, until thickened. Add the meatballs. Bring to a boil, cover, and cook, stirring gently once or twice, for about 30 minutes. Makes about 40–45 meatballs, or 7–8 servings.

# Lemon-Parsley Meatballs

1 pound ground beef
⅔ cup chopped parsley
½ cup fine dry bread crumbs
⅓ cup chopped onion
¼ cup milk
¾ teaspoon salt
¼ teaspoon each pepper and thyme
¼ teaspoon grated lemon peel
2 tablespoons oil
1 tablespoon lemon juice
1 tablespoon cornstarch

In a large bowl mix together the beef, parsley, bread crumbs, onion, milk, salt, pepper, thyme and lemon peel. Shape into balls and brown on all sides in hot oil. Add 1 cup water. Cover and simmer for 10 minutes. Stir together ½ cup water, the lemon juice and the cornstarch. Add to the skillet; bring to a boil; cook and stir for 1 minute. Makes 4 servings.

# Meatballs with Cranberry Gravy

1 pound ground beef
1 teaspoon marjoram, crumbled
1 beef bouillon cube dissolved in ¼ cup hot water
1 egg
1 cup soft bread crumbs
¼ cup wheat germ
¼ teaspoon steak sauce
Salt and pepper
Flour
2 tablespoons butter
1 cup cranberry juice
2 teaspoons minced parsley

Mix the beef, marjoram, bouillon, egg, bread crumbs, wheat germ, steak sauce, ½ teaspoon salt and ¼ teaspoon pepper. Shape into 12 balls, roll in flour and brown on all sides in the butter in a skillet. Remove the balls and blend 1½ tablespoons flour into the butter in the skillet, adding a little more butter if necessary. Cook for a few minutes, then add the cranberry juice and parsley. Bring to a boil and cook, stirring, until thickened. Add the meatballs and simmer until heated through, adding salt and pepper to taste. Makes 4 servings.

# Meatballs with Apple and Onion Sauce

*Sweet and spicy.*

1½ pounds ground beef
⅓ cup chopped onion
1 egg
2 slices white bread, crumbled in ⅓ cup milk
2 teaspoons salt
Flour
Oil
2 onions, sliced
2 medium apples, cored and sliced
½ cup raisins
⅔ cup water
¼ cup cornstarch
1 cup beef bouillon
⅓ cup molasses
1½ teaspoons packed brown sugar
4 teaspoons vinegar
½ teaspoon ground ginger

Mix the beef, chopped onion, egg, bread with milk, and 1 teaspoon of the salt. Form into small balls. Dip in the flour; brown in a small amount of hot oil in a large skillet. Add the sliced onions and apples and sauté for 5 minutes. Add the raisins and water. Cover and cook over low heat for 15–20 minutes. Remove the meatballs and keep warm. Blend the cornstarch with the beef bouillon. Pour into a skillet and add the molasses, the remaining 1 teaspoon salt, brown sugar, vinegar and ginger. Cook over low heat until thickened. Add the meatballs and heat through. Makes 6–7 servings.

# Wine Meatballs with Raisin Sauce

¼ cup fine dry bread crumbs
⅓ cup milk
1½ pounds ground beef
1 egg
1 teaspoon salt
⅛ teaspoon pepper
2 tablespoons minced onion
1 tablespoon butter
1½ tablespoons flour
1 garlic clove, crushed
1 cup condensed beef broth or consommé
2 tablespoons tomato paste
½ cup seedless raisins
¼ cup red table wine
Salt and pepper

Soak the bread crumbs in the milk, then mix with the beef, egg, salt, pepper and 1 tablespoon of the minced onion. Shape into 1½-inch balls and brown on all sides in butter in a skillet. Remove the meatballs. Blend the flour and crushed garlic with the drippings in skillet and cook for a minute or two. Add the remaining 1 tablespoon onion, broth, tomato paste, raisins and meatballs. Cover and simmer for 10 minutes. Remove the meatballs to a hot serving dish. Stir the wine into the sauce in the skillet and season to taste with salt and pepper. Pour over the meatballs and serve. Makes 5–6 servings.

# Applesauce Meatballs in Cider Sauce

*An autumn dish if there ever was one. Serve with acorn squash and biscuits for a truly seasonal meal.*

1 cup soft bread crumbs
½ cup unsweetened applesauce
1 pound ground beef
¼ pound ground pork
¼ pound ground veal
½ cup finely chopped onion
1 egg, beaten
1½ teaspoons salt
¼ teaspoon white pepper
⅛ teaspoon nutmeg
¼ teaspoon cloves
Flour
Butter
1 cup beef bouillon
1 cup cider
2 teaspoons cornstarch

Mix the bread crumbs and the applesauce. Combine the meats, then mix them with the onion, egg and the bread crumbs and applesauce. Add the seasonings and mix well. Shape into 2-inch balls and roll each ball lightly in flour. Heat 3 tablespoons of butter in a large, heavy skillet. Brown the balls for 5–10 minutes, shaking the pan frequently. Add the bouillon and cider. Cover and simmer for 30 minutes. Transfer the balls to a heated serving dish with a slotted spoon. Blend the cornstarch with 1 tablespoon of cold water and stir this into the sauce with a fork. Bring the sauce to a boil, taste for seasoning, and strain over the balls. Makes 6 servings.

Note: 1½ pounds ground beef can be substituted for the beef-pork-veal mixture.

## Meatballs with Oriental Sauce

*There's orange marmalade in the sauce, and peanut butter too!*

**1 pound ground beef**
**3 slices white bread, crusts removed**
**1 egg**
**2 tablespoons prepared horseradish**
**½ teaspoon salt**
**1 can (5 ounces) water chestnuts, drained and chopped**
**½ cup water**
**Oriental Sauce (see next page)**

Mix all the ingredients except the Oriental Sauce. Shape into 18 small balls and put in a greased baking pan. Bake in a preheated 350° F. oven for 15–20 minutes. Serve hot with Oriental Sauce. Makes 4 servings.

ORIENTAL SAUCE

¾ cup orange marmalade
1 clove garlic, minced
3 tablespoons soy sauce
1½ tablespoons lemon juice
¼ cup peanut butter
3 tablespoons water

Put all ingredients in a saucepan and bring to a boil, stirring until blended. Makes 1¼ cups.

# Sweet and Sour Meatballs

*Cook this a day or two in advance. It is even tastier when allowed to sit in the refrigerator for a few days.*

1½ pounds ground beef
1 egg
½ cup milk
¼ cup fine dry bread crumbs
1½ teaspoons salt
¼ teaspoon pepper
3–4 tablespoons butter
Sweet and Sour Sauce ( see next page )
1 teaspoon cornstarch blended with 1 tablespoon water

Mix well the beef, egg, milk, bread crumbs, salt and pepper. Shape into 1-inch meatballs. Heat the butter in a skillet, then brown the meatballs, about a third at a time, removing them as done. Return all meatballs to the skillet and add the Sweet and Sour Sauce. Bring to a boil, then cover and simmer for 30 minutes. Stir in the blended cornstarch; cook, stirring, until slightly thickened and smooth. Makes 6 servings.

SWEET AND SOUR SAUCE

1 cup hot water
½ cup raisins
2 tablespoons butter
2 tablespoons cider vinegar
2 tablespoons catsup
2 tablespoons packed brown sugar
1 bay leaf
8 peppercorns
1 teaspoon ground ginger
½ teaspoon salt

Mix all the ingredients thoroughly. Makes about 2 cups.

# Sweet and Sour Meatballs with Red Cabbage

1 medium onion, minced
1 tablespoon butter
½ cup vinegar
1 teaspoon caraway seeds
3 cloves
1 bay leaf
1 pound ground beef
1 egg
¼ cup fine dry bread crumbs
¼ cup chopped raisins
¼ teaspoon nutmeg
1½ teaspoons salt
½ teaspoon pepper
4 cups chopped red cabbage
2 tablespoons packed brown sugar
1 tart apple, peeled and diced

In a large saucepan or Dutch oven cook the onion in butter for 5 minutes. Add the vinegar, caraway seeds, cloves and bay leaf; cover and simmer for 5 minutes. Mix the beef, egg, bread crumbs, raisins, nutmeg, 1 teaspoon of the salt and ¼ teaspoon of the pepper. Shape into 16 balls. Add the meatballs to the first mixture and cook, stirring with a fork, for a few minutes. Remove the meatballs from the pan. Mix the cabbage, brown sugar, apple, the remaining ½ teaspoon salt and ¼ teaspoon pepper. Put the cabbage mixture in the bottom of the saucepan. Add the meatballs. Cover and simmer for 45 minutes. Put the meatballs in a serving dish and surround with the cabbage. Makes 4 servings.

# Meatballs in Cucumber Sauce

*An old Scandinavian favorite.*

1 cup soft bread crumbs
¾ cup dry white wine
1 pound ground beef
½ cup finely chopped onion
1 egg, slightly beaten
Salt and pepper
Flour
5 tablespoons butter
3 medium cucumbers
1 small onion, sliced thin
3 cups chicken broth
Dill
8–10 boiled potatoes

Combine the bread crumbs, ¼ cup of the wine, the beef, chopped onion, egg, 1 teaspoon of salt and ¼ teaspoon of pepper. Mix very well and shape into 16 balls, each about 2 inches. Roll each ball in flour. Sauté the balls in 1 tablespoon of the butter for 3 minutes, shaking the pan frequently. Pare and halve the cucumbers, scooping out the seeds with a spoon. Cut the cucumbers in small chunks. Heat the remaining butter in a deep saucepan. Add the sliced onion and sauté until soft. Stir in 4 tablespoons of flour and, when blended, stir in the broth and the remaining wine. Stir until slightly thickened. Add the cucumbers and cook for 10 minutes over medium heat. Add the meatballs and cook for 10 minutes longer. Season to taste with salt and pepper and a teaspoon of dill. Serve on a heated platter surrounded by dill-sprinkled boiled potatoes. Makes 4 servings.

# Meatballs with Sauerkraut

1 can (27 ounces) sauerkraut, drained
3 tablespoons caraway seeds
2 tablespoons honey
About 20 meatballs (see Basic Meatballs #1
    and #2, pp. 141 and 142)
Salt and pepper

Mix well the sauerkraut, caraway seeds and honey in a large skillet. Add the meatballs and cook, stirring occasionally, over low heat for 15–25 minutes, or until the meatballs are heated through. Season to taste with salt and pepper. Makes 5 servings.

# Swedish Meatballs

1 medium onion, minced
Butter
1 cup dry bread crumbs
1 cup milk
2 eggs, beaten
1 pound ground beef
½ pound ground pork
½ pound ground veal
1 teaspoon salt
½ teaspoon pepper
¼ teaspoon nutmeg
3 tablespoons flour
2 cups beef broth or consommé
Pinch of grated lemon rind
1 cup sour cream
Chopped dillweed or parsley

Sauté the onion in 1 tablespoon of butter until golden. Combine the bread crumbs, milk and eggs and let stand for a few minutes, then combine with the meats, onion, salt, pepper and nutmeg. Shape this mixture into small balls. Brown the meatballs in 2 tablespoons of butter, then remove them from pan. Blend the flour into the pan drippings and cook for a minute or two, then add the broth and cook, stirring, until slightly thickened. Add the lemon rind and meatballs. Bring to a boil and simmer, covered, over very low heat for 45 minutes. Remove the meatballs to a serving dish. Stir the sour cream into gravy in the skillet and heat gently. Pour over the meatballs and sprinkle with fresh dillweed. Makes 6–7 servings.

# Meatball Kebabs

*Not your run-of-the-mill outdoor barbecue fare, these are unusual and delicious.*

2 pounds ground beef
½ teaspoon ground cloves
⅛ teaspoon crushed cardamom seeds
¼ teaspoon pepper
⅛ teaspoon cayenne
½ teaspoon ground ginger
½ teaspoon cumin
2 teaspoons salt
1 heaping tablespoon sour cream
1 large onion, chopped
12 mushrooms
2 green peppers, in chunks

Mix all the ingredients except the mushrooms and green pepper chunks. Shape into 16 meatballs. Place on skewers, alternating the meatballs with the mushrooms and pepper chunks. Cook over a charcoal grill (or broil in the oven) to desired doneness. Makes 7–8 servings.

# Meatball Curry

*Curries are at their best when accompanied by such condiments as chutney, chopped egg, raisins, shredded coconut, peanuts, chopped green pepper and diced cucumber. Serve these in small bowls and let everyone help himself.*

1 pound ground beef
½ cup soft bread crumbs
1 egg, slightly beaten
1 teaspoon ground ginger
1½ teaspoons salt
¼ teaspoon pepper
1 small onion, minced
1 clove garlic, minced
2 tablespoons butter
1 tablespoon curry powder
2 tablespoons flour
Dash of cayenne
2 cups milk
1 package (10 ounces) frozen peas, thawed

Combine the meat with the bread crumbs and ¼ cup water. Mix the egg with the ginger, ½ teaspoon of the salt and the pepper and add this to the meat. Mix lightly and shape into 24 small meatballs. In a large skillet cook the onion and garlic in the butter until tender. Stir in the curry powder, flour, remaining 1 teaspoon salt and the cayenne. Add the milk and cook, stirring, until thickened. Add the meatballs, bring to a boil and simmer, covered, for about 15 minutes. Add the peas and cook for a few minutes longer, or until the peas are tender. Makes 5–6 servings.

# Meatballs, East Indian-Style

*Serve with curry condiments, especially chutney, shredded coconut and chopped hard-cooked egg.*

2 tablespoons butter
1 large onion, chopped
¾ teaspoon cinnamon
¼ teaspoon mace
1 teaspoon curry powder
1½ teaspoons peppercorns (in a cheesecloth bag)
½ cup seedless raisins
¼ cup slivered blanched almonds
1½ cups water
1 teaspoon salt
½ cup soft bread crumbs
¼ cup milk
1 pound ground beef
3 tablespoons chopped parsley
1 egg
1 teaspoon Worcestershire sauce
½ teaspoon pepper

Heat the butter in a large skillet. Reserving 2 tablespoons of the onion for the meat mixture, cook the onion until lightly browned. Add the seasonings, raisins, almonds and water. Cover and simmer for 15 minutes. Remove the peppercorns bag. Mix together the remaining ingredients and shape into small balls. In a second skillet brown the balls on all sides, using a small amount of butter if needed. Drain off any excess fat and add the meatballs to the first mixture. Cover and simmer for 20 minutes. Makes 4 servings.

## Spanish Meatballs

1½ pounds ground beef
1 tablespoon finely chopped parsley
½ teaspoon salt
½ teaspoon white pepper
⅛ teaspoon nutmeg
½ cup chopped onion
1½ cups beef bouillon
1 pound fresh peas, shelled
2 tomatoes, chopped
3 pimientos, chopped
2 teaspoons brandy
2 cloves garlic, crushed

Mix well the beef, parsley, salt, pepper and nutmeg and shape this mixture into small balls. Bake on a rack in a shallow pan in a preheated 350° F. oven for 15 minutes, or until done, turning once. In a saucepan cook the onion in ½ cup of the bouillon over low heat for 5 minutes, or until just tender. Stir in the remaining ingredients and add the meatballs. Simmer for 5–7 minutes, or until the peas are done. Makes 5–6 servings.

# Meatballs with Creole Sauce

*Serve over hot, buttered grits.*

2 tablespoons butter
¼ pound mushrooms, sliced
½ cup finely chopped green pepper
1 small onion, chopped fine
2 cloves garlic, crushed
1 can (15 ounces) tomato puree
½ teaspoon salt
¼ teaspoon pepper
16 meatballs (see Basic Meatballs #1 and #2,
    pp. 141 and 142)

Heat the butter in a saucepan and add the mushrooms, green pepper, onion and garlic. Cook, stirring frequently, until the onions and peppers are limp. Add the tomato puree, salt and pepper and simmer gently for 20–30 minutes. Add the meatballs and cook for about 15 minutes, or until heated through. Makes 4 servings.

---

# Meatballs with Barbecue Sauce

---

*Serve over a bed of rice and pour the wonderful sauce over all.*

1 can (16 ounces) tomatoes, undrained
2 medium onions, chopped fine
2 cloves garlic, crushed
½ cup cider vinegar
¼ cup packed brown sugar
¼ cup molasses
1 tablespoon Worcestershire sauce
¼ teaspoon hot pepper sauce
16 meatballs (see Basic Meatballs #1 and #2,
   pp. 141 and 142)

Whirl the tomatoes, onions and garlic in a blender. Stir in the vinegar, brown sugar and molasses. Pour this mixture into a saucepan and simmer for about 1½ hours. Add the Worcestershire sauce, hot pepper sauce and meatballs and simmer for 30 minutes more, or until the meatballs are heated through. Makes 4 servings.

# Barbecued Meatballs and Baked Beans

1 pound ground beef
1 teaspoon salt
¼ teaspoon pepper
⅓ cup fine dry bread crumbs
¾ cup water
Butter
¼ cup catsup
2 tablespoons brown sugar
2 tablespoons vinegar
2 teaspoons Worcestershire sauce
1 teaspoon prepared mustard
2 cans ( 16 ounces each ) beans with pork

Mix the beef, salt, pepper, bread crumbs and water. Shape into small balls, each about 1½ inches in diameter. Brown the balls in butter in a skillet over medium heat, then pour off the fat. Add the remaining ingredients except the beans; simmer for 5 minutes. Add the beans and put everything in a 1½-quart casserole. Bake in a preheated 350° F. oven for 25 minutes, or until hot and bubbly. Makes 4 servings.

# Meatballs in Sugo di Carne

*Serve with hot, buttered fettucine.*

1 pound ground beef
2 tablespoons olive oil
2 tablespoons flour
½ cup finely chopped mushrooms
¼ cup finely chopped onion
2 tablespoons tomato paste
1 cup beef broth
1 teaspoon salt
½ teaspoon pepper

Shape the beef into 15 balls, each about 1 inch in diameter. In a cast-iron or other heavy skillet heat the olive oil over medium heat. Dust the meatballs with flour and brown them in the hot oil on all sides for about 5 minutes. Remove the meatballs and drain off most of the fat. Add the mushrooms and onion to the pan and sauté for 2–3 minutes. Mix the tomato paste and broth and add this to the skillet. Season with salt and pepper and mix well. Put the meatballs back in the skillet and simmer gently for 15 minutes. Makes 4 servings.

# Chili Meatballs

1 pound ground beef
¼ cup white cornmeal
1 clove garlic, minced
1 small onion, grated
1 teaspoon coriander
1 teaspoon salt
¼ teaspoon pepper
Chili Sauce (see below)

Lightly mix all the ingredients except the Chili Sauce. Shape into balls, each about ¾ inch in diameter. Drop into boiling Chili Sauce, cover and simmer for 10–15 minutes. Makes 4 servings.

CHILI SAUCE

1 tablespoon butter
1 small onion, chopped
1 clove garlic, minced
1–2 tablespoons chili powder
1 can (18 ounces) tomato juice
Salt and pepper

Melt the butter in a large saucepan. Add the onion and garlic and cook slowly until lightly browned. Add the chili powder and tomato juice and simmer for 10 minutes. Season with salt and pepper to taste.

# Deviled Meatballs

*Served on toothpicks, these meatballs make wonderful hors d'oeuvres.*

½ pound ground beef
¾ teaspoon soy sauce
1 teaspoon prepared mustard
1 teaspoon catsup
½ teaspoon Worcestershire sauce
¼ teaspoon salt
¼ teaspoon garlic salt

Mix all the ingredients lightly. Shape into 16 small balls. Sauté slowly in a skillet until the meatballs are browned and done. Serve warm or cold.

# Savory Meatballs in Gravy

2 pounds ground beef
3 tablespoons minced onion
2 teaspoons salt
¼ teaspoon each pepper and nutmeg
2 eggs
Flour
2 tablespoons butter
2 cups beef bouillon
1 bay leaf

Mix the beef, onion, salt, pepper, nutmeg and eggs. Shape into 2-inch balls and roll in flour. Brown on all sides in the butter in a skillet. Add 1½ cups of the bouillon and the bay leaf. Bring to a boil, cover and simmer for 30 minutes. Mix ¼ cup flour with the remaining ½ cup bouillon until smooth. Stir into the mixture and cook, stirring gently, until thickened. Remove the bay leaf. Makes 7–8 servings.

# Hamburger Stroganoff

*The classic beef, mushrooms and sour-cream dish made with hamburger.*

2 pounds ground beef
¼ cup soft bread crumbs
1 clove garlic, minced
¼ cup water
1 egg
1 large onion, sliced
½ pound mushrooms, chopped
4 tablespoons oil
2 tablespoons flour
2 cups water
2 beef bouillon cubes
¼ cup sherry
2 tablespoons tomato paste
1 teaspoon dry mustard
1 cup sour cream

Mix the beef, bread crumbs, garlic, water and egg. Shape into 1-to-1½-inch balls. Cook the onion and mushrooms in 3 tablespoons of the oil until lightly browned. Remove the onion and mushrooms. Add the remaining 1 tablespoon oil, heat and brown the meatballs on all sides. Remove the meatballs. Add the flour to the skillet and brown this well.. Add water, bouillon, sherry, tomato paste and mustard; cook, stirring, until smooth and thickened. Add the meatballs, onion and mushrooms; simmer, uncovered, for about 15 minutes. Just before serving, blend in the sour cream. Makes 7–8 servings.

# Meatballs Jardinière

2 pounds ground beef
1 cup soft bread crumbs
1 cup applesauce
1 egg
2 teaspoons salt
¼ teaspoon allspice
¼ teaspoon pepper
½ cup flour
3 tablespoons oil
1 cup sliced carrots, partially cooked
1 small onion, sliced
1 small green pepper, chopped
2 cups tomato juice

Mix lightly but thoroughly the beef, bread crumbs, applesauce, egg, salt, allspice and pepper. Shape into 1½-inch balls, roll these in the flour and brown them on all sides in the oil in a skillet. Put the meatballs in a 3-quart casserole and add the remaining ingredients to the drippings in the skillet. Bring to a boil, scraping up the brown bits in the bottom of the skillet. Pour over the meatballs, cover and bake in preheated 350° F. oven for about 45 minutes. Makes 7–8 servings.

# Meatballs with Onion-Tomato-Pea Sauce

1½ pounds ground beef
1 cup stale bread crumbs
2 eggs, slightly beaten
½ cup freshly grated Parmesan cheese
½ cup raisins
½ cup chopped parsley
½ cup milk
1 small onion, minced
1½ teaspoons salt
½ teaspoon thyme
¼ teaspoon pepper
Onion-Tomato-Pea Sauce (see next page)

In a mixing bowl combine all the ingredients except the sauce. Mix thoroughly and shape into 18 balls, each 2 inches in diameter. Broil the meatballs on a broiler rack about 6 inches from the heat for 6 minutes, turning once. Remove to a 3-quart casserole. Pour the Onion-Tomato-Pea Sauce over the meatballs. Cover and bake in preheated 300° F. oven for 30 minutes. Makes 6 servings.

ONION-TOMATO-PEA SAUCE

3 tablespoons oil
3 medium onions, chopped
1 clove garlic, minced
3 large ripe tomatoes, peeled, seeded and chopped;
    or 1 can (16 ounces) tomatoes, drained
1 teaspoon oregano
1 package (10 ounces) frozen peas, thawed

Heat the oil in a heavy saucepan and sauté the onions and
garlic, stirring occasionally, for about 6 minutes. Add the
tomatoes and oregano. Cover and simmer for 10 minutes.
Stir in the peas and simmer for 6 minutes more.


# Eggplant-Meatball Casserole

1 pound ground beef
½ cup chopped onion
1 teaspoon salt
½ teaspoon pepper
2 tablespoons catsup
⅓ cup olive oil
Flour
1 medium eggplant, in ¾-inch-thick slices
2 cups Tomato Sauce (p. 263)
Chopped parsley (optional)

Mix together the beef, onion, salt, pepper and catsup.
Shape into about 24 balls the size of walnuts. Heat 1 tablespoon of the olive oil in a heavy skillet and sauté the

meatballs over fairly high heat until well browned. Rub flour onto the surfaces of the eggplant slices. In another large skillet, heat the remaining olive oil and brown the eggplant on both sides. Transfer to a 12-by-8-by-2-inch baking dish and top with the browned meatballs. Pour the Tomato Sauce over the top. Bake in a preheated 400° F. oven for about 15 minutes, or until hot and bubbly. Sprinkle with parsley if desired. Makes 4 servings.

# MEAT LOAVES

EVERYONE KNOWS that meat loaves are economical and easy to prepare. But not everyone realizes how very diverse they are. Delicious both hot and cold, there are many different ways to prepare them and countless sauces that, served over a basic meat loaf, work very special magic (see pp. 261–278).

You can vary a basic meat loaf recipe just by adding a favorite seasoning while you prepare it—some steak sauce, Worcestershire sauce, lemon juice, hot pepper sauce, crushed garlic or grated cheese. Try tossing in some chopped celery, nuts, parsley, green or black olives, mushrooms, green peppers or pimientos. Don't be timid about experimenting or using your imagination—meat loaf is *that* kind of food.

Use very lean ground meat for meat loaf and always drain off the fat after the meat loaf has cooked. Meat loaf mixture—a combination of ground beef, pork and veal sold in many meat markets and supermarkets—can usually be substituted for ground beef.

Always mix meat loaf ingredients lightly, just enough to incorporate them into each other. Overmixing tends to make the loaves tough and rubbery.

If you are in a hurry, you can divide the meat into small ovals and bake them in a baking dish for about half the baking time given in the recipe.

If you let meat loaves stand for five to ten minutes before removing them from the baking pan, they will be easier to cut. (They are even easier to slice when cold, of course.) It's also good to let a meat loaf sit for a while so that any remaining liquid in the pan will be absorbed and the loaf itself will be juicier.

Always try to make two meat loaves, even when you need only one. The recipes are easy to double, and you can serve one hot one day and the other cold the next. Or freeze one and reheat it later. It is better, by the way, to freeze meat loaf *after* baking than before.

To freeze meat loaf, wrap the loaves airtight, using freezer-weight aluminum foil or plastic wrap. You can also use polyethylene bags, but squeeze out all the air before fastening them. Label the wrapped loaves, noting the kind of loaf it is and when it was baked.

Reheat meat loaves in a preheated 325° to 350° F. oven, heating only to serving temperature. Do not overcook them. Or simply thaw the loaves and serve them at room temperature, maybe in sandwiches.

# Basic Meat Loaf

*There are innumerable ways to dress up a plain meat loaf.*
*For inspiration, turn to Sauces for Ground Meat Dishes,*
*pp. 261–278.*

2 eggs
1 cup beef, chicken or vegetable broth
¾ cup fine fresh bread crumbs
1 tablespoon minced onion
2 teaspoons salt
1 teaspoon crushed rosemary or preferred herb
½ teaspoon pepper
2 pounds ground beef

Beat the eggs in a mixing bowl, add the remaining ingredients in the order given and lightly mix. Shape into a
smooth loaf in a shallow baking pan and bake in a preheated 350° F. oven for 1 hour. Makes 7–8 servings.

## Speedy Meat Loaf

*One of the quickest-to-cook meat loaves we know. If you do not have a blender, chop the onions and parsley very fine, beat the egg slightly, then combine all the ingredients.*

1 medium onion, quartered
4 large sprigs of parsley
¾ cup milk
1 egg
¼ cup fine dry bread crumbs
1 teaspoon salt
½ teaspoon pepper
1½ teaspoons sugar
⅛ teaspoon allspice
½ pound mushrooms, chopped coarse
1½ pounds ground beef
1 cup Tomato Sauce ( p. 263 )

Combine the onion, parsley, milk, egg, bread crumbs, salt, pepper, sugar and allspice in a blender and whirl for a few seconds. Add to the mushrooms and beef and mix well. Pack into a 9-by-5-by-3-inch loaf pan and cover with Tomato Sauce. Bake in a preheated 375° F. oven for about 1¼ hours. Let stand for about 10 minutes before removing from the pan. Lift out with a pancake turner. Makes 6 servings.

# Family Meat Loaf

1½ pounds ground beef
¼ cup milk
1 egg, slightly beaten
4 tablespoons butter, melted
3 tablespoons chopped onion
2 tablespoons chopped parsley
4 tablespoons catsup
2 teaspoons salt
½ teaspoon pepper
6 strips bacon
Beef bouillon
2 tablespoons flour

Mix the meat, milk, egg, butter, onion, parsley, catsup, salt and pepper in a large bowl until thoroughly blended. Place the mixture in a large loaf tin and cover with bacon strips. Cover with aluminum foil and bake in a preheated 350° F. oven for 1 hour. Remove the foil and continue baking for 15 minutes. Remove the bacon and pour off the drippings from the loaf into a measuring cup. Add enough bouillon to measure 1¾ cups. Blend the flour with 4 tablespoons water. Combine with the bouillon sauce and bring to a boil, whisking until smooth and thickened. Pour this over the meat loaf and return to the oven for 30 minutes longer. Makes 6 servings.

Note: The meat loaf can be baked ahead of time and reheated for 45 minutes in the sauce.

## Party Meat-Loaf Roll

2 cups soft bread crumbs
½ cup finely chopped celery
½ teaspoon sage
¾ cup finely chopped onion
1½ teaspoons salt
1¼ teaspoons pepper
2 pounds ground beef
½ cup chili sauce
¼ cup corn relish
¼ pound mushrooms, sliced and sautéed
½ cup diced Cheddar cheese
1 tablespoon Worcestershire sauce
½ teaspoon salad herbs
2 tablespoons flour

Combine the bread crumbs, celery, sage, ¼ cup of the onion, ½ teaspoon of the salt, ¼ teaspoon of the pepper and ⅓ cup water and set aside. In a separate bowl combine the remaining ingredients except the flour and mix well. Shape the meat into a 14-by-9-inch rectangle on a sheet of waxed paper. Spread the first mixture on top of the meat. Roll up like a jelly roll by gently pulling the waxed paper up and over the meat and stuffing. Put in a shallow roasting pan and bake in a preheated 300° F. oven for about 1½ hours. Remove the meat from the pan and pour off all but 2 tablespoons of the fat. Remove the pan from the oven and stir in the flour. Add 1½ cups water and bring to a boil on top of the stove, scraping up the essence in the pan. Strain and season to taste. Pour over the roll and serve. Makes 6–8 servings.

# Peach-Glazed Meat Loaf

2 pounds ground beef
1½ cups soft bread crumbs
1 tablespoon minced onion
½ teaspoon basil
½ teaspoon marjoram
1½ teaspoons salt
¼ teaspoon pepper
1 egg, slightly beaten
1½ cups skim milk
1 can (30 ounces) sliced peaches, drained and syrup
  reserved
2 tablespoons white vinegar
2 tablespoons catsup
½ teaspoon paprika
1 teaspoon dry mustard
Canned peach halves
Parsley

Combine the meat, bread crumbs, onion, basil, marjoram, salt, pepper, egg and milk and mix well. Shape into a meat loaf in a shallow baking dish. Bake in a preheated 350° F. oven for 30 minutes. Meanwhile purée the sliced peaches and put them in a saucepan with the peach syrup, vinegar, catsup, paprika and dry mustard. Bring to a boil, reduce heat and simmer, stirring occasionally, for 15 minutes. Spoon part of this peach glaze on the loaf and bake for 30 minutes longer. Slice the meat loaf and serve with the remaining glaze spooned over the top and a garnish of peach halves and parsley. Makes 7–8 servings.

# Burgundy Meat Loaf

1½ pounds ground beef
1¼ cups Burgundy
½ cup chopped onion
¼ cup chopped celery
1 clove garlic, crushed
4 tablespoons butter
2 teaspoons salt
½ teaspoon pepper
¾ cup soft bread crumbs
¼ teaspoon nutmeg
½ cup chopped parsley
2 eggs, slightly beaten
¼ cup catsup
2 tablespoons packed brown sugar
2 teaspoons dry mustard

Combine the meat with 1 cup of the wine and let stand for 2 hours. Sauté the onion, celery, and garlic in the butter until the onions are soft. Add to the meat along with the salt, pepper, bread crumbs, nutmeg, parsley and eggs. Mix well. Place the mixture in a long loaf tin. Mix the catsup, brown sugar, mustard and the remaining ¼ cup of wine and spread this over the loaf. Bake for 1 hour in a pre-heated 350° F. oven. Let stand for 10 minutes before serving. Makes 6 servings.

# Hamburger and Egg Meat Loaf

*There's a special surprise inside this loaf. Use a sharp knife:*
*A slice of hard-cooked egg will appear in each serving.*

2 cups soft bread crumbs
½ cup milk
2 pounds ground beef
½ cup chopped onion
1 clove garlic, crushed
2 eggs, slightly beaten
½ teaspoon thyme
2 tablespoons parsley
2 teaspoons salt
½ teaspoon pepper
4 hard-cooked eggs
1 teaspoon Dijon mustard
2 tablespoons mayonnaise
Seasoned salt
Ten-Minute Tomato Sauce (p. 264), heated

Soak the bread crumbs for a few minutes in the milk and
squeeze dry. Combine this with the beef. Add the onion,
garlic, eggs and seasonings and mix thoroughly. Halve the
hard-cooked eggs and remove the yolks. Mash the yolks
well with the mustard and mayonnaise; season highly with
seasoned salt. Stuff the egg whites with the yolk mixture
and put the egg halves back together again. Cut off the
tips of the whites. Line a buttered loaf tin with three-
quarters of the meat mixture. Lay the eggs end to end
on the meat and cover with the remaining meat mixture.
Pour half of the Ten-Minute Tomato Sauce over the loaf.

Bake for 1¼ hours in a preheated 350° F. oven. Let stand for 10 minutes before turning out onto a heated platter. Serve the rest of the sauce in a separate bowl. Makes 8 servings.

## Sausage-Stuffed Meat Loaf

2 pounds ground beef
2 teaspoons salt
¼ teaspoon pepper
2 eggs
½ cup soft bread crumbs
½ cup milk
¼ cup finely chopped onion
¼ teaspoon each marjoram and poultry seasoning
¼ pound small breakfast sausages, panfried until browned
3 strips bacon
Meat-Mushroom Sauce (p. 266), optional

Combine all the ingredients except the sausages, bacon and sauce and mix well. Pack half into a 9-by-5-by-3-inch loaf pan. Arrange the sausages in two rows on top. Pack in the remaining mixture. Cover with bacon strips. Bake in a preheated 350° F. oven for about 1 hour and 10 minutes. Let stand for a few minutes, then pour off the liquid and remove the loaf with a large turner to a platter. Slice and serve plain or with Meat-Mushroom Sauce. Makes 6–8 servings.

# Liver-Meat Loaf

3 pounds ground beef
½ cup finely chopped onion
2 tablespoons butter
1 cup soft bread crumbs
1 scallion (green onion), sliced thin
2 tablespoons finely chopped celery tops
2 eggs, slightly beaten
½ cup light cream or milk
1½ teaspoons thyme
2 teaspoons salt
½ teaspoon pepper
6 chicken livers, parboiled and diced
2 tablespoons prepared mustard
1 cup beef bouillon

Put the beef in a large bowl. Sauté the onion in the butter for a few minutes. Mix the onion, meat, bread crumbs, scallion, celery, eggs, cream and seasonings. Gently stir in the chicken livers. Shape into a loaf in a 13-by-9-by-2-inch shallow baking pan, making a loaf the length of the pan. Spread with the mustard. Bake in a preheated 375° F. oven for 10 minutes. Pour the bouillon over the top and bake, basting every 15 minutes with the broth in the pan, for 1 hour and 10 minutes longer. Serve hot with gravy made from the pan drippings. Makes 10–12 servings.

## Specialty Meat Loaf

*This special meat loaf should be served cold.*

½ cup fine dry bread crumbs
1½ cups milk
1 tablespoon minced onion
2 pounds ground beef
2 eggs, slightly beaten
2 tablespoons chili sauce
2 teaspoons salt
Freshly ground black pepper
1 teaspoon ground ginger
1 teaspoon curry powder
1 tablespoon prepared horseradish
⅓ cup pine nuts
3 tablespoons capers, drained
1 jar (4 ounces) pimientos, drained and cut up

Mix the bread crumbs, milk and onion and let stand. Put the meat in a large bowl and add the remaining ingredients except the capers and pimientos. Then add the bread crumb mixture and mix well. Gently stir in the capers and pimientos. Line a 13-by-9-by-2-inch pan with foil. Shape the meat into a loaf about as long as the pan and bake in a preheated 350° F. oven for 1 hour. Cool, then chill. Makes 7–8 servings.

# Piquant Meat Loaf

2 eggs
1 cup beef broth
⅔ cup fine fresh bread crumbs
2 tablespoons minced onions
2 teaspoons salt
1 teaspoon basil
½ teaspoon pepper
2 pounds ground beef
¼ cup catsup
2 tablespoons molasses
2 tablespoons vinegar
1 tablespoon prepared mustard
1½ teaspoons Worcestershire sauce
Dash of hot pepper sauce

Beat the eggs in a large bowl and add the broth, bread crumbs, onion, salt, basil, pepper and beef. Mix lightly with your hands. Shape into a smooth loaf in a shallow baking pan. Blend together the catsup, molasses, vinegar, mustard, Worcestershire sauce and hot pepper sauce. Spread this sauce mixture over the meat loaf. Bake in a preheated 350° F. oven for 1 hour. Makes 7–8 servings.

# Savory Meat Loaf

Fine dry bread crumbs
2 cups milk
½ cup chopped onion
1½ tablespoons butter, melted
2 pounds ground beef
1 cup grated carrot
2 eggs
2 tablespoons chili sauce
2 teaspoons salt
2 teaspoons anchovy paste
1 teaspoon ground ginger
1 teaspoon curry powder
Freshly ground black pepper
Prepared mustard

Mix ⅔ cup crumbs, the milk and onion in a bowl and let stand for a few minutes. Add the remaining ingredients except the mustard. Mix well and shape into a loaf in a shallow baking dish. Spread a thin layer of mustard over the loaf and sprinkle with bread crumbs. Bake in a pre-heated 350° F. oven for 1 hour, or until done. Makes 7–8 servings.

# Savory Meat Loaf with Celery Sauce

2 pounds ground beef
½ cup fine soft bread crumbs
1 medium onion, chopped fine
1 large rib celery with top, chopped fine
1 medium clove garlic, crushed
2 teaspoons salt
½ teaspoon rosemary
½ cup milk
2 eggs, slightly beaten
1 tablespoon butter
Celery Sauce (see below)

In a bowl mix well all the ingredients except the butter
and Celery Sauce. Pack into a 9-by-5-by-3-inch loaf pan
and dot with the butter. Bake in a preheated 350° F. oven
for 1 hour, or until done. Remove from the pan with 2
spatulas, reserving the drippings for the Celery Sauce.
Serve with the sauce. Makes 6–8 servings.

CELERY SAUCE

Milk
1 large celery rib, sliced
1 small onion, sliced thin
1 tablespoon butter
1 tablespoon flour
¼ teaspoon salt
¼ teaspoon rosemary

Strain the reserved drippings into a large measuring cup. Add enough milk to make 1 cup. In a small saucepan sauté the celery and onion in the butter until tender. Blend in the flour, salt and rosemary, and cook over medium heat, stirring, until hot and bubbly. Gradually stir in the milk mixture. Cook, stirring, until the mixture thickens and begins to boil. Makes about 1¼ cups.

## Casserole Meat Loaf

1 pound ground beef
¼ cup finely chopped onion
½ cup finely chopped celery
1¼ teaspoons salt
½ teaspoon pepper
1 tablespoon prepared mustard
3 tablespoons chopped stuffed olives
1 cup cooked rice
¾ cup milk

Combine all the ingredients and mix well. Put in a 1½-quart casserole. Bake in a preheated 375° F. oven for about 45 minutes. Cut into wedges and serve. Makes 4 servings.

# Rice Meat Loaf

1 cup cooked rice
1 pound ground beef
2 eggs, well beaten
⅓ cup minced onion
2 tablespoons minced green pepper
1½ teaspoons salt
1 teaspoon Worcestershire sauce
1 teaspoon curry powder
1 cup Tomato Sauce (p. 263)
2 teaspoons prepared mustard

Combine the rice, beef, eggs, onion, green pepper, salt, Worcestershire sauce, curry powder and ½ cup of the Tomato Sauce. Form into a loaf and place in a baking pan. Spread the surface with mustard and top with the remaining sauce. Bake in a preheated 350° F. oven for 1 hour. Makes 4 servings.

# Sauerbraten Meat Loaf

*The famous German dish Sauerbraten that inspired this meat loaf recipe is traditionally served with potato dumplings or potato pancakes. Many people prefer simpler accompaniments such as boiled potatoes or noodles.*

2 pounds ground beef
1 cup soft bread crumbs
1 cup crushed gingersnaps
½ cup chopped onion
½ cup beer
⅓ cup vinegar
2 eggs, slightly beaten
2 teaspoons salt
¼ teaspoon pepper
⅛ teaspoon ground cloves
Steak sauce

Mix all the ingredients except steak sauce. Shape into 11-by-4-inch loaf on a broiler pan. Brush with the steak sauce. Bake in a preheated 350° F. oven for about 1½ hours. Let stand for 10 minutes before slicing. Makes 7–8 servings.

# Individual Stroganoff Meat Loaves

½ cup sour cream
1 pound ground beef
1 cup fine cracker crumbs
¼ cup chopped mushrooms, sautéed in butter
1 tablespoon tomato paste
2 tablespoons chopped parsley
¼ cup chopped onion
1 egg
½ teaspoon salt
⅛ teaspoon pepper
Steak sauce
Snipped dillweed (optional)

Mix well ⅓ cup of the sour cream and all the remaining ingredients except the steak sauce and dillweed. Divide into 3 equal portions and shape into oval loaves. Place on a rack in a broiler pan and brush with the steak sauce. Bake in a preheated 350° F. oven for about 40–50 minutes. Top each loaf with a dollop of sour cream and sprinkle with dillweed. Makes 3 servings.

## African-Style Meat Loaf

*This lightly fruity loaf is wonderful served with mango chutney and sliced bananas, pineapple spears and apple slices. And don't forget to serve rice.*

2 medium onions, chopped
1 large firm apple, peeled and diced
2 tablespoons butter
2 tablespoons dry sherry or Sauterne
2 teaspoons curry powder
1 cup fine bread crumbs (made from toast)
½ cup milk
2 pounds ground beef
2 teaspoons salt
¼ teaspoon pepper
2 dashes hot pepper sauce
2 eggs, lightly beaten
2 tablespoons apricot or pineapple preserves, or orange marmalade
½ cup salted peanuts, chopped fine
½ cup Tomato Sauce (p. 263)

Sauté the onion and apple in the butter in a small skillet until golden. Remove from the heat and stir in the sherry and curry powder. Put the bread crumbs in a large bowl, add the milk and mix well. Then stir in the beef, salt, pepper, hot pepper sauce and the curry mixture. Add the remaining ingredients except the Tomato Sauce and mix lightly but thoroughly. Put in a 9-by-5-by-3-inch loaf pan and bake in a preheated 350° F. oven for 45 minutes. Remove from the oven and drizzle Tomato Sauce over the top. Bake for 15 minutes longer. Let stand in the pan for 15 minutes before turning out onto a platter. Makes 8 servings.

# South-of-the-Border Meat Loaves

2 pounds each ground beef and ground pork
2 cups milk
2 cups soft bread crumbs
2 cloves garlic, minced
2 teaspoons salt
½ teaspoon pepper
¼ teaspoon dry mustard
2 teaspoons poultry seasoning
⅛ teaspoon ground cloves
½ pound chorizos or hot Italian sausage
1½ cups chopped raw spinach
4 hard-cooked eggs, sliced
4 strips bacon
1 cup Tomato Sauce (p. 263)

Mix the meats, milk, bread crumbs, garlic, salt, pepper, mustard, poultry seasoning and cloves lightly but thoroughly. Divide into 4 even parts. Shape 2 parts into two 11-by-6-inch loaves in a baking pan. Sauté the sausage until cooked but still soft; crumble. Pat the sausage, chopped spinach and egg slices on the shaped loaves and cover with the remaining meat, forming firm loaves. Cut the bacon strips in half and lay them at an angle on meat loaves. Pour the Tomato Sauce over the tops. Bake in a preheated 350° F. oven for about 1 hour. Let stand for 10 minutes before removing from the pan. Each loaf makes 8–10 servings.

## Spanish-Style Meat Loaf

1½ cups canned chick-peas, well-drained and mashed
1½ pounds ground beef
3 eggs
½ cup tomato juice
1 small green pepper, chopped
1 medium onion, minced
2 pimientos, chopped
½–1 teaspoon oregano, crumbled
1½ teaspoons salt
Dash of hot pepper sauce

Combine all the ingredients in a large mixing bowl and, with your hands, mix lightly but thoroughly. Pack in a 9-by-5-by-3-inch loaf pan and bake in a preheated 350° F. oven for 1 hour. Cool and chill in the pan. Unmold and serve in thin slices with salads or in sandwiches. Makes 7–8 servings.

# Italian Meat Loaf

*Serving this with spaghetti and sauce is a must.*

1½ pounds ground beef
½ pound ground pork or Italian sausage meat
2 cups soft bread crumbs
½ cup tomato juice
½ cup chopped onion
2 eggs
2 teaspoons salt
¾ teaspoon oregano
¼ cup chopped parsley
¼ cup freshly grated Parmesan cheese
Chopped parsley for garnish

Mix together all the ingredients except the chopped parsley for garnish. Form into a 9-by-5-inch oval loaf in a greased baking pan. Bake in a preheated 350° F. oven for 1 hour and 20 minutes. Let stand for 10 minutes before slicing. Garnish with chopped parsley. Makes 6–8 servings.

## Meat Loaf with Ricotta Cheese

*The cheese makes a sauce for the meat loaf. Spoon it over the sliced meat when serving.*

1 pound ground beef
1 cup soft bread crumbs
3 eggs
½ cup grated Romano or Parmesan cheese
1 tablespoon minced onion
¼ cup water
1 tablespoon chopped parsley
1¼ teaspoons chopped fresh basil or ½ teaspoon dried
1¾ teaspoons salt
¼ teaspoon pepper
1 tablespoon olive or other oil
2 tablespoons fine dry bread crumbs
½ pound ricotta cheese

Mix together the meat, bread crumbs, 2 of the eggs, Romano or Parmesan cheese, onion, water, parsley, 1 teaspoon of the basil, 1½ teaspoons of the salt and the pepper. Brush the inside of a 9-by-5-by-3-inch loaf pan with the oil. Sprinkle with the fine dry crumbs. Pat half of the meat mixture into the pan. Mix the ricotta cheese with the remaining egg, ¼ teaspoon basil and ¼ teaspoon salt. Spread over the meat. Pat out the remaining meat and press on top of the cheese. Bake in a preheated 350° F. oven for 1 hour, or until done. Makes 4–5 servings.

# Blue-Cheese Meat Loaf

*Wonderful served cold, too.*

2 tablespoons butter
1 medium onion, chopped
1 green pepper, chopped
½ cup chili sauce
3 tablespoons water
1½ pounds ground beef
¼ pound sweet Italian sausage meat
½ teaspoon salt
½ teaspoon sage
½ teaspoon Dijon mustard
¼ teaspoon pepper
2 cups fine dry bread crumbs
1 cup milk
2 eggs, slightly beaten
¾ cup (4 ounces) crumbled blue cheese

Heat the butter in a skillet and add the onion and green pepper; cook for about 5 minutes. Add ¼ cup of the chili sauce and the water and cook for 4 minutes more. Pour this mixture into a 9-by-5-by-3-inch loaf pan. Mix the remaining ¼ cup chili sauce with the rest of the ingredients. Press into the pan on top of the onion-pepper mixture. Bake in a preheated 375° F. oven for about 1½ hours. Makes 6 servings.

# MEAT PIES

✧᳝✧᳝✧᳝✧᳝✧᳝✧᳝✧᳝✧᳝✧᳝✧᳝✧᳝✧᳝✧᳝✧᳝✧᳝✧᳝✧᳝✧᳝✧᳝✧᳝

❖❥❖❥❖❥❖❥❖❥❖❥❖❥❖❥❖❥❖❥❖❥❖❥❖❥❖❥❖❥❖❥❖❥

FEW CAN DENY that a hot, steaming meat pie is a delight to see, smell and taste. But many cooks avoid meat pies, considering them too difficult to make. In reality, meat pies are no more complicated than any casserole you might prepare.

If you are wary of mixing your own pie pastry, you can use a pastry mix or thaw a frozen pie shell. But it is really very easy and gratifying to make pie pastry yourself, using your own favorite method or our simple, basic pie pastry recipe (see next page). And the result is so delicious!

You can freeze a meat pie either before or after baking. Wrap it tightly in freezer-weight aluminum foil, noting on the label what kind of pie it is, how many servings it will provide and when it was prepared or baked. Unbaked pies will keep for up to six months in your freezer; baked pies should be used within two to three months.

Reheat frozen unbaked meat pies, without defrosting them, in a preheated 350° F. oven, adding an extra forty-five minutes or so to the baking time and keeping the pie covered for the first half hour so that the crust does not end up being too brown. Baked frozen meat pies can also be reheated from a frozen state or allowed to defrost, uncovered, then heated until crisp in a preheated 350° F. oven.

# Basic Pie Pastry

2 cups flour
1 teaspoon salt
⅔ cup shortening or ½ cup lard
4–5 tablespoons ice water

Mix the flour and salt. Cut in the shortening, using a pastry blender or your fingers. Add ice water a few drops at a time, mixing with a fork and using only enough water to get the dough into a ball. Makes enough for one 2-crust 8- or 9-inch pie or 2 pie shells.

# Beef-Squash Pie

Pastry for one 2-crust pie
Fine dry bread crumbs
2 pounds butternut squash, peeled and diced
2 tablespoons vinegar
1 pound ground beef
½ cup minced onion
1 cup grated Cheddar cheese
Salt, pepper and basil
½ cup cream
1 tablespoon butter
1 egg yolk, slightly beaten

Roll out about two-thirds of the pastry and line a shallow 2-quart baking dish with it. Sprinkle lightly with bread crumbs. Put the diced squash in a saucepan and add a small amount of water plus the vinegar. Bring to a boil and simmer, covered, until tender; drain. Sauté the beef and onion until the meat loses its red color, breaking up the meat with a fork as it cooks. Drain off excess fat. In the baking dish alternate layers of squash, cheese and the meat mixture, ending with squash and reserving some cheese for the top. Season each layer well with salt, pepper and basil. Pour cream over the top, sprinkle with the reserved cheese and dot with butter. Roll out the remaining pastry, cut it in strips and arrange them, lattice fashion, on top. Brush with slightly beaten egg yolk and bake in a preheated 350° F. oven for about 1 hour. Makes 6 servings.

## Canadian Hamburger Pie

Pastry for one 2-crust pie
½ cup grated sharp Cheddar cheese
½ teaspoon paprika
Dash of cayenne
1½ pounds ground beef
1 small onion, minced
1½ cups dry bread crumbs
Beef broth
½ teaspoon each salt and pepper
¼ teaspoon each thyme and marjoram
2 teaspoons Worcestershire sauce

When preparing the pastry dough, add the cheese, paprika and cayenne before adding liquid. Roll out half of the pastry and fit it in a 9-inch pie pan. Cook the beef and onion in a skillet until the meat loses its red color, breaking up the meat with a fork as it cooks. Drain off excess fat. Mix the bread crumbs and enough broth to moisten well and let stand for a few minutes. Add the beef mixture and the remaining ingredients. Mix well and pour into the pie shell. Roll out the remaining pastry and put it over the top, crimping edges and cutting a few slits for the steam to escape. Bake in a preheated 375° F. oven for about 45 minutes. Serve warm or cold. Makes 6 servings.

## Hamburger and Kidney Pie

*A variation of the old English favorite.*

1 beef kidney
1 tablespoon fat
2 cups boiling water
1 pound ground beef
1 medium onion, chopped
2 tablespoons flour
¼ cup cold water
1½ teaspoons salt
¼ teaspoon pepper
1 teaspoon steak sauce
Pastry for 1 pie shell

Cut the kidney in crosswise slices, remove the fat and gristle, then cut the kidney in small pieces. Rinse in cold water and wipe dry. Brown on all sides in the fat. Add the boiling water, cover and simmer for 1 hour, or until tender. Meanwhile cook the beef and onion, stirring with a fork, until the meat loses its red color. Add the cooked kidney and liquid. Blend the flour with the cold water and stir into the mixture. Cook until slightly thickened, stirring. Add the seasonings and pour into a 1-quart casserole. Roll out the pastry to a ⅛-inch thickness and cut it in strips. Arrange these on top of the mixture, lattice fashion. Bake in a preheated 400° F. oven for 20 minutes, or until the pastry is browned. Makes 4 servings.

## Finnish-Style Meat Pie

Pastry for one 2-crust pie
½ cup minced onion
½ cup minced mushrooms
2 tablespoons butter
1½ pounds ground beef
1 teaspoon salt
Milk
½ cup minced parsley
½ cup grated sharp Cheddar cheese
2 egg yolks
¼ teaspoon white pepper
Sour cream and cranberry sauce (optional)

Mix the pastry for the piecrust, wrap in plastic and chill while making the meat filling. Sauté the onion and mushrooms in the butter for a few minutes. Add the meat and sauté, stirring to break up the meat, for 20 minutes, or until all the liquid is evaporated. Pour into a mixing bowl and cool. Add the salt, ¼ cup of milk, parsley, cheese, 1 of the egg yolks and the pepper and mix well. Divide the pastry into two equal parts. Roll it out on a lightly floured board in two 10-by-6-inch rectangles. Cut the edges even with a pastry wheel and save the scraps for decoration. Put one pastry rectangle on a greased baking pan. Put the meat mixture on top and shape it into a loaf, using your hands, leaving a pastry border of about 1 inch all around. Cover with the remaining pastry rectangle and crimp the edges with a fork dipped in flour. Prick the entire loaf with a fork and decorate with strips of leftover pastry. Brush with milk (or the remaining egg yolk beaten with milk) and bake in a preheated 375° F. oven for 35–40 minutes. Slice and serve, warm or cool, with sour cream and cranberry sauce. Makes 6–8 servings.

## Spanish Beef Pies

1 tablespoon butter
1 large onion, chopped
½ green pepper, chopped
½ pound ground beef
¼ teaspoon salt
Pepper
½ cup canned corn, drained
¼ cup raisins
¼ cup chopped pitted olives
Pastry for two 2-crust pies
12 slices hard-cooked eggs (about 2 eggs)
1 egg white, slightly beaten

Heat the butter in a skillet; add the onion and green pepper and cook until both are lightly browned. Add the beef and cook until the meat loses its red color. Pour off any excess fat. Add the salt, pepper, corn, raisins and olives and mix well. Prepare the piecrust; divide the dough into 4 sections and roll each to a ⅛-inch thickness. Cut twelve 6-inch rounds by tracing a saucer. Put a spoonful of meat mixture onto half of each round and top with a slice of egg. Brush the edges with cold water and fold each pie in half, crimping the edges with a fork. Cut a few slits in the top for the steam to escape. Brush with the slightly beaten egg white. Bake in a preheated 450° F. oven for 15 minutes. Makes 12 pies, or 6 servings.

# Tamale Pie

*This is a southwestern adaptation of the familiar tamales served in Mexico since Aztec times.*

1 cup yellow cornmeal
3 cups well-seasoned beef or chicken broth, heated
1 pound ground beef
2 tablespoons shortening
1 clove garlic, minced
1 medium onion, chopped
1 small green pepper, chopped
1–2 tablespoons chili powder
1 can (16 ounces) tomatoes, undrained
1 can (12 ounces) whole-kernel corn, drained
Salt
¼ cup freshly grated Parmesan cheese (optional)

Mix the cornmeal and 1 cup of cold water in a heavy saucepan. Add the broth, stirring. Cook over low heat, stirring occasionally, for 10–15 minutes, or until the mixture has thickened. While the cornmeal is cooking, brown the beef in hot shortening in a large skillet, crumbling it with a fork. Add the garlic, onion, green pepper, and sauté for 5 minutes longer. Add the chili powder, tomatoes, corn and salt. Cover and simmer for 20 minutes. Spread half the cornmeal mixture on the bottom of a greased shallow 3-quart baking dish. Add the meat mixture and top with the remaining cornmeal. Sprinkle with Parmesan cheese if desired. Bake in a preheated 350° F. oven for 35 minutes, or until very hot. Makes 6 servings.

# Cheese-Topped Beef-Bean Pie

*For a Mexican touch, add one or two canned green chilies, chopped.*

Pastry for one 2-crust pie
1 pound ground beef
2 tablespoons butter
1 medium onion, minced
½ teaspoon salt
¼ teaspoon seasoned pepper
½ teaspoon chili powder
1 teaspoon Worcestershire sauce
1 can (16 ounces) pinto or red kidney beans, drained
1 egg, beaten
Cheese Topping (see next page)

Roll out the pastry for the piecrust, and line the bottom and sides of a 2-quart casserole with it. Sauté the meat in the butter in a skillet until it loses its red color, breaking it up with a fork. Drain off excess fat. Add the onion and seasonings and cook 1–2 minutes. Add the beans and egg and pour the mixture into the lined casserole. Bake in a preheated 425° F. oven for 20 minutes. Reduce the oven temperature to 350° F. Pour the Cheese Topping over the mixture in the casserole, making sure the edges are covered. Bake for 30 minutes, or until the topping is lightly browned. Makes 6–8 servings.

CHEESE TOPPING

2 tablespoons butter
2 tablespoons flour
½ cup milk
1 cup grated Cheddar cheese
2 eggs, separated

Melt the butter in the top part of a small double boiler. Blend in the flour. Gradually add the milk and cook, stirring, until thickened. Remove from the heat and add the cheese, stirring until melted. Slightly beat the egg yolks and stir them in. Beat the egg whites until stiff, then lightly fold them in.

# Beef Shepherd's Pie

2 tablespoons butter
¾ cup chopped onion
1½ pounds ground beef
1 cup thinly sliced carrots
1 teaspoon salt
1 tablespoon flour
2½ tablespoons Worcestershire sauce
1 package (10 ounces) frozen peas, thawed
2½ cups hot seasoned mashed potatoes

Heat the butter in a large skillet. Add the onion and sauté for about 5 minutes. Add the beef and sauté for 5 minutes longer. Add the carrots, ¼ cup water and the salt. Bring to a boil and reduce the heat. Cover and simmer for 10 minutes. Blend the flour with the Worcestershire sauce and stir this into the meat mixture. Add the peas, cover and simmer for 5 minutes. Pour into a 2-quart casserole. Cover with the mashed potatoes and make lengthwise and crosswise markings in the top with a fork. Bake in a preheated 400° F. oven for 20 minutes, or until golden. Makes 6 servings.

# Italian Ground Beef Pie

*The crust for this unusual pie is made of celery, croutons and grated Parmesan cheese.*

¾ cup chopped celery
2 tablespoons butter
1½ cups croutons
4 tablespoons freshly grated Parmesan cheese
1 egg, slightly beaten
1 pound ground beef
4 tablespoons chopped onion
1 clove garlic, minced
4 tablespoons catsup
1 teaspoon oregano
1 teaspoon salt
¼ teaspoon pepper
½ cup sliced mozzarella cheese

Sauté the chopped celery in the butter for 5 minutes, stirring frequently. Remove from the heat and stir in the croutons, Parmesan cheese and egg. Spread this mixture over the bottom of a buttered 9-inch pie pan. Mix the beef, onion, garlic, catsup, oregano, salt and pepper. Place on top of the "crust" in the pie pan. Bake in a preheated 350° F. oven for 30 minutes. Remove from the oven and turn the heat up to 400° F. Spoon out any excess fat from the pie and cover with the mozzarella slices. Return to the oven for 5 minutes, or until the cheese is melted and bubbling. Makes 4–5 servings.

# Pizza

*Reusable foil pizza pans are available at low cost.*

2½–3 cups flour
1½ teaspoons sugar
Salt
1 package active dry yeast
2 tablespoons oil
4 cups shredded cheese (mozzarella, Muenster, process
  Swiss or Cheddar)
2 cups Tomato Sauce (p. 263)
½ teaspoon oregano
¾ pound ground beef, browned and drained
Pepper
¾ pound pork sausage meat, browned and drained
½ cup freshly grated Parmesan cheese

To make the dough, mix thoroughly in the large bowl of an electric mixer 1 cup of the flour, the sugar, 2 teaspoons of salt and the yeast. Gradually add 1 cup very hot tap water and the oil and beat at the low speed of the electric mixer, scraping the bowl occasionally, for 1 minute. With a spoon, stir in enough additional flour to make a soft dough. Turn out onto a lightly floured board and knead for 8 minutes, or until the dough is smooth and elastic. Put in a greased bowl, turning to grease the top. Cover and let rise in a warm place for 45 minutes, or until doubled. Punch down and divide in half. Press each half into a greased 14-inch pizza pan, making the crust very thin and building it up on the ungreased rim of the pan to hold the edges. Sprinkle each pizza with the shredded cheese. Mix the Tomato Sauce and oregano and spread half of this on each pizza. Sprinkle one pie with the ground beef and season with salt and pepper. Sprinkle the other with sausage. Top both with grated Parmesan cheese. Bake in an extremely hot 500° F. oven for 20 minutes, or until the cheese is well browned and the crust is crisp. Serve at once. Makes two 14-inch pizzas.

# GROUND MEAT
## with PASTA

❂⟩❂⟩❂⟩❂⟩❂⟩❂⟩❂⟩❂⟩❂⟩❂⟩❂⟩❂⟩❂⟩❂⟩❂⟩❂⟩❂⟩❂⟩❂⟩❂⟩❂⟩❂⟩❂⟩❂⟩

CLEVER COOKS have mixed pasta with meat for as long as we can remember. What better way to stretch a small amount of meat and to enliven essentially bland pasta!

Pasta and ground beef dishes are generally one-dish meals; all that is needed for balance is a crisp green salad or vegetable on the side.

Don't be afraid to experiment with pasta dishes, to substitute one kind of pasta for another. Try spirals, shells, bows, zitis—or any of the many, many different kinds of macaronis available these days.

When freezing pasta dishes, bear in mind that certain seasonings increase in strength after freezing, especially black pepper, garlic, green pepper, pimiento and celery. Use these seasonings lightly if you plan to freeze a dish. Salt, onion and chili powder, on the other hand, almost disappear after freezing, so you may want to add a good deal more of these when reheating a frozen pasta dish.

You can freeze pasta dishes either before they have been cooked or after. Store them in plastic containers or as you would a casserole (see pp. 17–18) or in a baking dish covered with aluminum foil. Always label the containers, indicating the number of servings each dish contains and when it was prepared.

Pasta dishes will keep in the freezer for three to six months. Reheat them in a preheated 325° to 350° F. oven; reheating times will vary with each dish. It's best to heat pasta dishes from a frozen state, adding up to an hour to the regular baking time. Let pasta dishes bubble for ten to fifteen minutes before removing them from the oven.

# Beef-Macaroni Casserole

*The Italians may have invented macaroni, but what can be a more all-American dish than a beef and macaroni casserole?*

½ pound uncooked elbow macaroni
Salt
½ medium onion
1 medium green pepper
1 hot Italian sausage link
8 ounces Cheddar cheese
1 clove garlic, minced
¼ cup butter
½ teaspoon pepper
1 pound ground beef
Pinch of oregano
1 large bay leaf
1 can (8 ounces) tomatoes, undrained

Cook the macaroni in boiling salted water until tender; drain and set aside. Force the onion, green pepper, sausage and cheese through the medium blade of a good chopper and put the mixture in a saucepan with ¼ teaspoon salt and the rest of the ingredients. Cook slowly for 20 minutes. Spread the bottom of a 2-quart casserole with a layer of macaroni. Add the cooked mixture, then top with the remaining macaroni. Bake, uncovered, in a preheated 350° F. oven for about 30 minutes. Makes 6 servings.

## Spicy Beef-Macaroni Casserole

*Ample for a late-night party.*

¼ cup oil
2 large onions, sliced
1 pound ground beef
2 cans (16 ounces each) tomatoes
1½ teaspoons salt
1 clove garlic, minced
¼ teaspoon pepper
1 teaspoon hot pepper sauce
2 teaspoons Worcestershire sauce
1 teaspoon rosemary
1 teaspoon parsley
½ teaspoon celery seeds
½ pound Cheddar cheese, grated
1 cup milk
1 can (10½ ounces) condensed cream of mushroom soup
1 pound uncooked small shell macaroni
¼ cup cracker crumbs or fine dry bread crumbs

Heat the oil in a large skillet, add the onions and brown lightly. Add the beef and cook, stirring with a fork, until the meat loses its red color. Add the tomatoes and seasonings. Bring to a boil and simmer. Meanwhile in a saucepan over low heat melt the cheese in the milk and soup. In another pot, cook the macaroni; drain. Mix all the ingredients except the crumbs and divide the mixture among two 2-quart casseroles. Sprinkle each casserole with crumbs and bake in a preheated 350° F. oven for 35–40 minutes, or until browned and bubbly. Makes 10–12 servings.

# Chili-Beef Dinner

1 pound ground beef
1 small onion, chopped
1 medium clove garlic, minced
1 teaspoon each salt and chili powder
1 can (16 ounces) tomatoes, cut up, undrained
1 can (6 ounces) tomato paste
2 cups water
1 cup uncooked elbow macaroni

In a skillet brown the beef, breaking it up with a fork as it cooks; drain off any excess fat. Stir in the onion, garlic, salt, chili powder, tomatoes, tomato paste and water. Bring to a boil. Gradually stir in the macaroni so that the mixture continues to boil. Cover and simmer for 15 minutes, stirring occasionally. Remove the cover and simmer for 10 minutes, or until the sauce is thickened and the macaroni is tender. Makes 6 servings.

## Country-Style Beef and Macaroni

8 ounces uncooked macaroni
1 tablespoon butter
2 medium onions, sliced
1 clove garlic, minced
1 pound ground beef
½ teaspoon chili powder
1 jar (4 ounces) pimiento, drained and chopped
1 can (20 ounces) red kidney beans, drained
1 package (10 ounces) frozen peas, cooked and drained
Salt and pepper

Cook and drain the macaroni. Melt the butter and add
the onions, garlic, beef and chili powder. Cook over medium heat, stirring occasionally, until the beef is browned.
Drain off excess fat. Add the macaroni and the remaining
ingredients. Mix well and heat to serving temperature.
Makes 6–8 servings.

# Ground Beef and Spinach Casserole

1 pound ground beef
1 medium onion, chopped
¼ cup chopped celery
1 clove garlic, minced
½ pound shell macaroni, cooked and drained
1 package (10 ounces) frozen chopped spinach, thawed
½ cup shredded Swiss cheese
¾ cup milk
1 teaspoon salt
½ teaspoon rosemary
¼ teaspoon pepper

Cook the beef, onion, celery and garlic in a large skillet, stirring occasionally, until the meat is browned and the vegetables are tender. Drain off excess fat. In a large bowl combine the meat mixture with all the remaining ingredients. Turn this into a 2-quart casserole. Cover and bake in a preheated 350° F. oven for 30 minutes, or until hot. Makes 6 servings.

# Baked Macaroni with Ricotta

½ pound ground beef
1 clove garlic, minced
4 cups Tomato Sauce (p. 263)
2 tablespoons chopped parsley
1 teaspoon basil
1 teaspoon salt
½ teaspoon oregano
Freshly ground black pepper
3 cups cooked macaroni
1 container (15 ounces) ricotta cheese or 1 container
    (16 ounces) cottage cheese
½ cup shredded mozzarella cheese
Freshly grated Parmesan cheese

In a skillet brown the beef lightly, stirring to break it up;
drain off any excess fat. Add the garlic and sauté for a few
minutes, or until tender. Stir in the Tomato Sauce, parsley,
basil, salt, oregano and pepper and simmer, uncovered,
for 15 minutes. Combine this sauce, the macaroni and the
ricotta cheese in a 2-quart baking dish. Top with the
mozzarella and Parmesan cheeses, cover and bake in a preheated 350° F. oven for 20 minutes. Uncover and bake for
10 minutes longer, or until hot and bubbly. Makes 4–6
servings.

# Creole Meat-Loaf and Macaroni

This is the dish to make when you're tired of leftover meat loaf.

1 onion, minced
½ green pepper, minced
2 tablespoons butter
1 can (28 ounces) tomatoes, undrained
1¼ cups uncooked elbow or broken macaroni
1 cup water
1 bay leaf
1 teaspoon Worcestershire sauce
1–1½ cups leftover meat loaf, in bite-size pieces
Seasoned salt and pepper

Cook the onion and green pepper in the butter for 2–3 minutes. Add the tomatoes, macaroni, water, bay leaf and Worcestershire sauce. Bring to a boil and simmer, covered, for about 1 hour, or until the macaroni is tender, stirring frequently. Add the meat loaf pieces and heat. Season with salt and pepper to taste. Makes 4 servings.

# Greek Casserole

½ pound ground beef
1 medium onion, chopped
1 clove garlic, minced
1 can (16 ounces) tomatoes, cut up, undrained
½ teaspoon salt
¼ teaspoon pepper
⅛ teaspoon cinnamon
½ cup freshly grated Parmesan cheese
½ pound elbow macaroni, cooked and drained
3 tablespoons butter
⅓ cup flour
2¼ cups milk
3 eggs

In a large skillet cook the beef, onion and garlic until the meat is browned and the onion is tender, stirring occasionally. Drain off excess fat. Add the tomatoes, ¼ teaspoon of the salt, the pepper and cinnamon; simmer for 15 minutes. Stir in ¼ cup of the cheese and the macaroni. Turn into a 12-by-8-by-2-inch baking dish and set aside. In a medium saucepan melt the butter; blend in the flour and the remaining ¼ teaspoon salt. Gradually stir in the milk and cook, stirring, until the sauce thickens, about 5 minutes. Cool slightly. Beat in the eggs one at a time. Stir in the remaining ¼ cup cheese and pour over the meat mixture. Place in a preheated 400° F. oven, lower temperature to 375° F. and bake for 30–40 minutes, or until the top is golden brown and a knife inserted in the center comes out clean. Makes 6 servings.

# Skillet Quadrettini

1 pound ground beef
½ cup chopped celery
½ cup chopped onion
1 clove garlic, minced
1 teaspoon salt
1 teaspoon thyme
1 can (28 ounces) tomatoes, undrained, cut up
1 cup uncooked small shell macaroni
1 package (10 ounces) frozen chopped spinach, thawed

Brown the beef in a large skillet with the celery, onion and garlic, stirring to keep the meat crumbly. Drain off excess fat. Stir in the salt, thyme, tomatoes and macaroni. Bring to a boil, cover and simmer for 15–20 minutes, or until the macaroni is almost tender. Stir in the spinach, cover and cook for 5 minutes longer. Makes 4 servings.

## Spaghetti and Meatballs

1 pound ground beef
¾ cup rolled oats
1 teaspoon salt
¼ teaspoon pepper
1 egg
⅓ cup milk
2 tablespoons oil
1 large onion, chopped
1 clove garlic, minced
1 can (16 ounces) tomatoes, undrained
1 can (6 ounces) tomato paste
1¼ teaspoons oregano
½ teaspoon basil
¼ teaspoon pepper
⅛ teaspoon thyme
1 pound uncooked spaghetti

Combine the beef, oats, salt, pepper, egg and milk and
mix well. Shape into about 30 meatballs. Brown in the oil
in a large saucepan and then remove them from the pan.
Add the onion and garlic to the drippings and brown
lightly, stirring. Add the tomatoes, tomato paste, 1 cup of
water and the seasonings. Bring to a boil, add the browned
meatballs, cover and simmer for about 40 minutes. Cook
the spaghetti, and when it is done, serve topped with the
meatballs and sauce. Makes 6 servings.

# Spaghetti with Zucchini-Beef Sauce

1 pound ground beef
1 clove garlic, minced
1 pound small zucchini, sliced
1 cup diced green pepper
2 medium tomatoes, quartered
1 cup Tomato Sauce (p. 263)
1 teaspoon salt
¼ teaspoon pepper
¼ teaspoon each oregano and basil
½ pound uncooked spaghetti

Brown the beef and garlic in a skillet, stirring to break up the meat. Add the zucchini, green pepper, tomatoes and Tomato Sauce, and cook over medium heat for 5 minutes, or until it is all well mixed. Add the seasonings, cover and simmer for 30 minutes. Taste and correct the seasoning. Prepare the spaghetti as directed on the package. Serve the sauce over the hot spaghetti. Makes 4 servings.

# Baked Spaghetti with Chicken and Sausage Sauce

*The sausages add a spicy twist to this casserole—one of the great crowd-pleasers of all time.*

1 4-pound chicken
1 medium onion
1 stalk celery
1 carrot, in chunks
1½ teaspoons salt
4 sprigs of parsley
8 peppercorns
¼ pound butter
2 large onions, chopped fine
3 stalks celery, chopped fine
2 green peppers, chopped fine
5 cloves garlic, minced
1 can (16 ounces) tomatoes, undrained
½ pound mushrooms, sliced
¾ pound spicy Italian sausage
½ pound ground beef
2 bay leaves
¼ teaspoon crushed red pepper
¼ teaspoon thyme
¼ teaspoon basil
⅛ teaspoon pepper
½ cup flour
¼ cup heavy cream
1 pound spaghetti, cooked
½ pound sharp Cheddar cheese, shredded
Freshly grated Parmesan cheese

In a large pot place the chicken, onion, celery, carrot chunks, salt, parsley and peppercorns. Add water to a depth of ½ inch. Cover the pot and simmer for about 1 hour, or until the chicken is tender; set aside and cool, reserving the chicken broth. Heat 1 tablespoon butter in a large skillet and sauté the chopped onion, celery, green pepper and the minced garlic until tender. Put the tomatoes in a saucepan and add the onion-pepper mixture. Heat 3 tablespoons of the butter in the skillet used to sauté the onion-pepper mixture and sauté the mushrooms, stirring frequently, for about 3 minutes, until lightly browned. Add to the tomato mixture. Slice the sausages and brown them in the skillet. Discard the fat and add the sausage slices to the tomato mixture. Cook the ground beef in the same skillet, stirring with a fork, until it loses its red color. Remove with a slotted spoon and add to the tomato mixture together with the bay leaves, crushed red pepper, thyme, basil and pepper. Bring this sauce to a boil, then simmer for 20 minutes over low heat. Meanwhile drain the fat from the skillet, then melt the remaining 4 tablespoons of the butter in the skillet and stir in the flour. Cook for a few minutes, then add 3 cups of the reserved chicken broth and cook, stirring frequently, until the sauce thickens and boils. Stir in the cream. Combine the cream sauce with the tomato sauce. Cut the cooled chicken into small pieces, discarding the skin and bones. Grease a very large 6-quart casserole and cover the bottom with a little of the tomato sauce. Add a layer of the cooked spaghetti, then chicken pieces, following with a layer of Cheddar cheese. Repeat the layers until all the ingredients are used. Finish with a layer of Cheddar cheese. Bake, uncovered, in a preheated 400° F. oven for 30–40 minutes, or until bubbly. Serve with Parmesan cheese. Makes 10–12 servings.

# Stracotta with Linguine

Stracotta *means extra-long cooking. Perfect for people who like their pasta without tomato sauce.*

1 ounce dried mushrooms
½ cup dry Marsala or Madeira wine
Butter
1 pound ground beef
½ cup chopped onion
½ cup shredded carrot
1 stalk celery, minced
½ cup chopped parsley
1 cup beef bouillon
1 cup water
1 teaspoon grated lemon rind
1 teaspoon salt
¼ teaspoon pepper
1½ pounds uncooked linguine
Freshly grated Parmesan cheese (optional)

Soak the mushrooms in the wine. Heat some butter in a large skillet and sauté the beef, vegetables and parsley for 5 minutes, stirring with a fork to break up the meat. Add the mushrooms and wine, the bouillon, water, lemon rind and seasonings. Stir well, cover and simmer very slowly for 3–4 hours. Add more water if necessary. Just before serving, boil the linguine in a large kettle of salted water for 5–6 minutes, or until just tender. Drain, toss with a little butter and the *stracotta*. If desired, add grated Parmesan or Romano cheese, although that is not traditional. Makes 6 servings.

# Green Fettuccine with Meat-Mushroom Sauce

*There's a subtle richness to spinach noodles that regular noodles just do not have.*

1 pound green (spinach) fettuccine
Salt
¾ cup butter, softened
6 cups Meat-Mushroom Sauce (p. 266)
Freshly grated Parmesan cheese

Cook the fettuccine in boiling salted water until just tender. Drain well and toss with the butter. Top with sauce and a sprinkling of Parmesan cheese. Makes 5–6 servings.

# Cheese-Filled Manicotti with Meat Sauce

*A one-dish meal.*

2 pounds ricotta cheese or cottage cheese
½ pound mozzarella cheese, diced
2 eggs, well beaten
2 tablespoons chopped parsley
½ teaspoon pepper
¼ teaspoon nutmeg
½ cup slivered blanched almonds
Salt
1½ cups freshly grated Parmesan cheese
4 cups Meat-Mushroom Sauce (p. 266)
16 manicotti, cooked

Make the filling by mixing the ricotta cheese, mozzarella cheese, eggs, parsley, pepper, nutmeg, almonds, 1 teaspoon salt and 1 cup of the Parmesan cheese. Blend thoroughly. Bring the Meat-Mushroom Sauce to a boil. Spread ⅓ of the sauce in a large, shallow baking dish. Stuff the manicotti with the cheese filling and arrange in the baking dish. Cover with the remaining sauce and sprinkle with the remaining ½ cup Parmesan cheese. Bake in a preheated 350° F. oven for 20 minutes. Makes 6–8 servings.

## Meat-Filled Manicotti

1 tablespoon butter
½ pound ground beef
½ pound ground veal
½ pound ground pork
1 tablespoon minced onion
1 teaspoon grated lemon rind
½ teaspoon oregano
¼ teaspoon tabasco sauce
1 teaspoon salt
½ teaspoon pepper
2 eggs, well beaten
½ pound mozzarella cheese, diced
Brown Mushroom Sauce (p. 273)
16 manicotti, cooked
½ cup freshly grated Parmesan cheese

To make the filling, heat the butter in a large, heavy skillet. Lightly mix the beef, veal and pork with your hands, then add to the skillet and cook until browned, stirring with a fork. Drain off excess fat. Add the onion, lemon rind, seasonings, eggs and mozzarella cheese and set aside. Bring the Brown Mushroom Sauce to a boil. Spread one-third of the sauce in a large, shallow baking dish. Stuff the manicotti with the filling and arrange in the baking dish. Cover with the remaining sauce and sprinkle with Parmesan cheese. Bake in a preheated 350° F. oven for 20 minutes. Makes 6–8 servings.

## Lasagna

1 pound sweet or hot Italian sausage (in bulk, if available)
½ pound ground beef
1 can (16 ounces) tomatoes
2 cans (6 ounces each) tomato paste
1 tablespoon basil
1½ teaspoons salt
6 uncooked large, wide lasagna noodles
1 tablespoon olive oil
Cheese Filling (see next page)
1 pound mozzarella cheese, sliced thin

If the sausage is in links, remove the casing. Brown the meats in a skillet, breaking up the beef with a fork, and pour off the excess fat. Add the tomatoes, tomato paste, basil and salt; simmer, stirring occasionally, for about 30 minutes. Meanwhile cook the noodles in boiling salted water with the olive oil for about 15 minutes, or until just tender. Drain and arrange half the noodles in a 13-by-9-by-2-inch baking dish. Spread with half the Cheese Filling, then cover with half the mozzarella cheese slices, then half the meat sauce. Repeat the layers. Bake in a preheated 375° F. oven for about 30 minutes. Let stand for 10 minutes before cutting into squares. Makes 6–8 servings.

CHEESE FILLING

1 pound ricotta or cottage cheese
½ cup freshly grated Parmesan or Romano cheese
2 tablespoons snipped parsley
2 eggs, beaten
2 teaspoons salt
½ teaspoon pepper

Mix all the ingredients together.

## White Lasagna

1 pound ground beef
¾ cup minced onion
1 clove garlic, minced
1 teaspoon salt
⅛ teaspoon pepper
½ pound uncooked curly lasagna noodles
Cream Sauce (see next page)
1 pound ricotta cheese or cottage cheese
¾ cup freshly grated Parmesan cheese
½ pound mozzarella cheese, sliced
Chopped parsley

In a skillet cook the meat, breaking it up with a fork, for 2 minutes. Add the onion, garlic, salt and pepper and cook slowly, stirring often, for 5 minutes, or until the onions are limp. Cook the lasagna noodles as directed on the package, drain well and keep separated on waxed paper. Spread a small amount of Cream Sauce in a shallow baking dish about 13-by-8-by-2-inches. Add the remaining Cream Sauce to the meat mixture. Add a layer of noodles to the baking dish, spread with the meat sauce and dot with ricotta cheese. Then sprinkle with Parmesan cheese and top with a few slices of mozzarella. Repeat the layers, making 3 layers of each ingredient. Bake in a preheated 350° F. oven for 40 minutes, or until hot and bubbly. Let stand for about 5 minutes, then sprinkle with parsley. Makes 8 servings.

CREAM SAUCE

3 tablespoons butter
3 tablespoons flour
1 teaspoon salt
⅛ teaspoon pepper
Dash nutmeg
2½ cups milk
⅓ cup chopped parsley

Melt the butter in a saucepan and blend in the flour, salt, pepper and nutmeg. Cook for 2–3 minutes, then add the milk and cook, stirring, until thickened. Cook, stirring, for about 1 minute longer. Add the parsley.

# Rigatoni with Hamburger Sauce

1 pound ground beef
2 cloves garlic, minced
1 cup chopped onion
1 cup chopped celery
1 cup chopped green pepper
1 jar (4 ounces) pimientos, drained and diced
2 cups Tomato Sauce (p. 263)
½ cup freshly grated Parmesan cheese
2 cups diced sharp Cheddar cheese
1 pound rigatoni noodles, cooked and drained

Mix the beef, garlic, onion, celery, green pepper, pimientos, and Tomato Sauce in a saucepan and simmer, covered, stirring occasionally, for 1 hour. Stir in the cheeses and serve on the hot noodles. Makes 6 servings.

## Mazetti

*A great dish to take to potluck suppers.*

1 pound ground beef
½ pound wide egg noodles, cooked until almost tender,
  then drained
1 large onion, chopped
4 stalks celery, chopped
1 large garlic clove, minced
¼ pound mushrooms, chopped
2 tablespoons butter
1 can (12 ounces) corn, undrained
1 can (10½ ounces) condensed tomato soup
½ cup milk
1½ teaspoons salt
½ teaspoon pepper
½ pound Cheddar cheese, shredded

Brown the beef well in a large, heavy skillet over medium
heat, stirring occasionally to break it up; drain off excess
fat. Add the beef to the cooked noodles; set aside. In the
same skillet sauté the onion, celery, garlic and mushrooms
in the butter until the onion is tender, stirring occasionally.
Add to the beef-noodle mixture. Stir in the corn, condensed tomato soup, milk, salt and pepper until well
mixed. Turn into a greased 3-quart casserole. Sprinkle with
shredded Cheddar cheese. Bake, uncovered, in a preheated
400° F. oven for 25–30 minutes, or until hot and bubbly.
Makes 6–8 servings.

# Meatballs with Almond-Mushroom Noodles

1½ cups tomato puree
1 cup sour cream
1 pound ground beef
2 sprigs of parsley, chopped
1 teaspoon salt
⅛ teaspoon pepper
⅓ cup fine dry bread crumbs
1 egg
3 tablespoons butter
1 medium onion, minced
1 clove garlic, minced
1 bay leaf
1 teaspoon lemon juice
1 teaspoon paprika
2 cups uncooked wide noodles
¼ cup slivered almonds
¼ pound mushrooms, sliced

Mix the tomato puree and sour cream. Add ¼ cup of this mixture to the beef, parsley, salt, pepper, bread crumbs and egg; mix well. Shape into 16 small balls. Cook in 1 tablespoon of the butter until well browned. Remove the meatballs and cook the onion and garlic in the fat remaining in the skillet until lightly browned. Drain off any remaining fat. Add the meatballs, remaining sour cream mixture, bay leaf, lemon juice and paprika; bring to a boil, cover and simmer for 20 minutes. Uncover and cook for 10 minutes longer. Meanwhile cook and drain the noodles. Sauté the almonds and mushrooms slowly in the remaining

2 tablespoons butter until golden brown, stirring frequently. Mix with the noodles and arrange in a border on a hot platter. Put the meatballs and sauce in the center. Makes 4 servings.

## Noodle and Beef Skillet

1½ pounds ground beef
2 onions, minced
½ cup finely chopped green pepper
2 tablespoons butter
½ pound mushrooms, sliced
3 cups beef bouillon
3 tablespoons flour
¼ cup water
Dash of Tabasco sauce
1 teaspoon salt
Pepper
½ teaspoon thyme or basil
½ pound flat noodles, cooked

Cook the beef in a heavy skillet, adding a small amount of butter if necessary, until slightly browned, breaking it up with a fork as it cooks; set aside. Cook the onions and green pepper in 2 tablespoons of butter until soft. Add the mushrooms and sauté for 5 minutes, covered. Add the meat and cook for 5 minutes more. Add the bouillon and heat to boiling. Meanwhile mix the flour with the water into a smooth paste and add this to skillet when the contents are boiling. Stir in the seasonings and simmer for 15 minutes, stirring occasionally. Add the noodles and heat. Makes 6 servings.

# Beef, Noodle and Cheese Casserole

1 pound ground beef
2 cups Tomato Sauce (p. 263)
½ teaspoon oregano
Salt
½ pound uncooked wide noodles
1 cup ricotta or cottage cheese
8 ounces cream cheese
¼ teaspoon pepper
3 scallions (green onion), chopped
¼ cup sour cream

Cook the beef in a skillet until the meat loses its red color, breaking it up with a fork; drain off excess fat. Add the Tomato Sauce and oregano and heat. Bring 4 cups water and 1 tablespoon salt to a boil in a large saucepan. Cook the noodles and drain them. Put half the noodles in the bottom of a shallow baking dish. Mix together 1 teaspoon salt, the cheeses, pepper, scallions and sour cream. Spread this mixture on the noodles. Add the remaining noodles. Pour the meat mixture over the top. Bake in a preheated 350° F. oven for 30 minutes. Makes 6 servings.

# GROUND MEAT
## with RICE

❀❀❀❀❀❀❀❀❀❀❀❀❀❀❀❀❀❀❀❀❀❀❀❀❀❀❀❀

WHEN MAKING RICE, use the following guideline: One cup of uncooked rice will make about three cups of cooked rice. Minute rice, which takes less time to cook, has a lower yield: One cup of uncooked Minute rice will make about two cups of cooked rice.

Try substituting brown rice for white rice in any of these recipes. It's nutritious and adds character to many a dish. Brown rice will take somewhat longer to cook than white rice and also has a greater yield: One cup of uncooked brown rice will produce about four cups of cooked rice.

Standard one-half cup servings of rice often seem too skimpy. It's sensible to expect four servings from one cup of uncooked rice; it's always better to have some left over rather than not to have enough. And since most of the recipes in this chapter call for cooked rice anyway, you'll be happy to have leftover rice on hand. You can also mix leftover rice with freshly cooked rice, if you don't have enough for the recipe requirements.

Do not wash rice either before or after cooking, or much of its food value will be lost.

Most of these recipes can be prepared very quickly, so there is no point in freezing them, especially since rice tends to get somewhat soggy after it has been frozen.

# Hamburger-Rice Casserole

1 pound ground beef
½ cup chopped onion
1 clove garlic, minced
½ cup chopped green pepper
½ cup chopped celery
2½ cups chicken or beef broth
1 cup Tomato Sauce (p. 263)
2 eggs, well beaten
1½ cups uncooked rice
1½ teaspoons salt
½ teaspoon pepper
1 cup shredded Cheddar cheese

Cook the beef, onion, garlic, green pepper and celery in a skillet, stirring to break up the meat, until the meat loses its red color and the vegetables are tender. Combine the broth, Tomato Sauce and eggs and mix well. Add the rice, seasonings and half the cheese. Combine with the meat mixture in a 2-quart casserole, cover and bake in a preheated 350° F. oven for 1½–2 hours, or until the rice is tender and the liquid has been absorbed. Uncover, sprinkle with the remaining cheese and bake for 10 minutes longer, or until the cheese is melted. Makes 6 servings.

# Ground Beef with Beans and Rice

½–1 pound ground beef
1 small onion, chopped coarsely
1 clove garlic, minced
2 cans (16 ounces each) kidney or pinto beans, undrained
2 carrots, sliced thin
1½ teaspoons salt
⅛ teaspoon pepper
Cooked rice

In a skillet brown the beef lightly, stirring with a fork to break it up; drain off excess fat. Add the onion and garlic and cook, stirring, for about 5 minutes, or until the onion is tender. Stir in the beans, carrots, salt and pepper; cover and simmer for 25 minutes, or until the flavors are blended. Serve with rice. Makes 4–6 servings.

# Beef and Brown Rice Casserole

*The brown rice adds a special nutty flavor to this casserole.*

1 pound ground beef
1 cup sliced mushrooms
½ cup chopped onion
½ cup chopped green pepper
1 beef bouillon cube
½ cup uncooked brown rice
1 teaspoon salt
¼ teaspoon pepper
Freshly grated Parmesan cheese

Brown the beef, breaking it up with a fork; drain off any excess fat. Add the mushrooms, onion and green pepper and sauté with the beef until the onion is tender. Dissolve the bouillon cube in 1¾ cups boiling water and pour into a 1½-quart casserole. Stir in the rice, beef mixture and seasonings. Cover and bake in a preheated 375° F. oven for 1 hour. Uncover, sprinkle with the cheese and bake for 10–15 minutes longer, or until the rice is tender, the top is browned and the liquid completely absorbed. Makes 4 servings.

# Rice Pilaf with Meatballs

2 tablespoons butter
1 cup uncooked rice
1 can (10½ ounces) beef broth or consommé
⅛–¼ cup sliced scallions (green onion)
⅛ teaspoon nutmeg
½ cup cooked, fresh or partially thawed frozen green beans
12–16 meatballs (pp. 141–142)
Salt and pepper

Melt the butter in a Dutch oven. Add the rice and cook, stirring, for 3–5 minutes, or until the rice is transparent. Slowly pour in the broth, undiluted. Stir in the scallions and nutmeg. Add the green beans and meatballs. Cover and cook over low heat for about 20 minutes, or until the meatballs are heated through and the rice is tender. Set aside and let stand, covered, for 15 minutes. Gently fluff the rice before placing it in a serving dish. Season with salt and pepper to taste. Makes 4 servings.

# Beef-Pork-Rice Casserole

6 tablespoons minced onion
4 tablespoons butter
1 cup uncooked rice
Salt
¼ cup minced parsley
¾ cup soft bread crumbs
2½ cups milk
1 egg
Pepper
¼ teaspoon nutmeg
1½ pounds ground beef
½ pound ground pork
¼ cup flour
1 cup shredded Cheddar cheese

In a saucepan sauté 2 tablespoons of the onion in 2 table-spoons of the butter until golden. Add the rice, 2 cups water and 1 teaspoon salt. Cook until tender. Add the parsley and line the bottom and sides of a 3-quart casserole; set aside. Soften the bread crumbs in ½ cup of the milk. Add the egg, 2 teaspoons salt, ¼ teaspoon pepper and the nutmeg and beat with a fork until well mixed. Sauté the remaining onion in the remaining butter until golden. Add the sautéed onions along with the meat to the bread crumb mixture. Shape into 36 balls and brown them in a large skillet without added fat, transferring the meat-balls to the lined casserole as they brown. Drain off all but ¼ cup of the drippings. Blend the flour into the drippings. Add the remaining milk and cook, stirring, until smooth and thickened. Add the cheese and season with salt and pepper to taste. Pour the sauce over the meatballs and bake in a preheated 350° F. oven for about 20 minutes. Makes 8 servings.

# Winter Squash Baked with Beef-Rice Stuffing

3 medium acorn or butternut squashes
1 pound ground beef
½ cup chopped onion
½ teaspoon salt
Pepper
1 cup Tomato Sauce (p. 263)
2 teaspoons Worcestershire sauce
½ teaspoon thyme
2 cups cooked rice
½ cup shredded Cheddar cheese

Cut the squashes in half and remove the seeds. Put them, cut side down, in a shallow baking dish and add about ½ inch boiling water. Bake in a preheated 350° F. oven for 45 minutes, or until the squash is almost fork-tender. Meanwhile brown the beef in a skillet, stirring to break up the meat. Add the onion and cook until tender. Add the salt, pepper, Tomato Sauce, Worcestershire sauce and thyme and simmer for a few minutes. Stir in the cooked rice. Turn the squash cut side up and divide the meat-rice mixture evenly among the halves. Shape the filling into a mound. Add more boiling water to the pan if necessary. Put back in the oven and bake for 40 minutes. Sprinkle with cheese and bake for 10 minutes longer. Makes 6 servings.

# Ground Beef and Rice Skillet with Tomatoes and Raisins

*Raisins and tomatoes add an exotic touch to an old standby.*

1 pound ground beef
1 large onion, chopped
1 small green pepper, chopped
1 large clove garlic, minced
1 tablespoon oil
1 cup uncooked rice
¼ cup chopped raisins
2 tablespoons freshly grated Parmesan cheese
1½ teaspoons oregano
1¼ teaspoons salt
1 beef bouillon cube
1 can (16 ounces) tomatoes, undrained
1½ cups water
Green pepper strips (optional)

In a large skillet cook the beef, onion, chopped green pepper and garlic in the oil until the beef is browned. Stir in the remaining ingredients except the green pepper strips. Bring to a boil, reduce the heat, cover and simmer for about 30 minutes, or until the rice is tender and the liquid has been absorbed. Garnish with green pepper strips. Makes 4 servings.

## Far Eastern Rice and Beef

1 cup cooked rice
2 tablespoons butter
2 medium onions, sliced
½ green pepper, sliced
1 pound ground beef
1¼ teaspoons salt
1 tablespoon curry powder
½ cup seedless raisins
1 bay leaf
1 package (10 ounces) frozen peas
2 tablespoons cornstarch
½ cup salted peanuts

Put the rice in the bottom of a shallow 1½-quart baking dish. Melt the butter in a skillet, add the onions and green pepper and cook, stirring, for 5 minutes. Sprinkle the beef with the salt and curry powder and add to the skillet. Cook, stirring to break up the meat, until the meat loses its red color. Add the raisins, bay leaf and 1½ cups water and bring to a boil. Cover and simmer for about 5 minutes. Add the peas, cover and cook for 3–5 minutes, or until the peas are tender. Thicken with the cornstarch mixed with a little cold water. Pour the meat mixture over the rice and mix partially. Heat in a preheated 350° F. oven for 10–12 minutes. Sprinkle with the peanuts. Makes 4–6 servings.

# Middle Eastern Hamburger Steaks

*A tasty rice filling is tucked inside these patties.*

2 tablespoons seedless raisins
½ cup cooked rice
2 tablespoons minced scallions (green onion)
½ teaspoon salt
1 teaspoon curry powder
2 tablespoons mayonnaise
1½ pounds ground beef
Butter
Salt and pepper

To make the filling, pour a cup of boiling water over the raisins and let stand for 5 minutes, strain and mix with rice, scallions, salt, curry powder and mayonnaise. Spread the beef out into a large 16-by-8-inch rectangle. Cut into 4-inch squares (a ruler is helpful here). Cover half the meat squares with the filling, leaving a ¾-inch margin around the edges. Place the remaining squares on top and seal the edges, crimping them with your fingers. Place the steaks on a lightly buttered broiling pan and broil for 6–8 minutes, turning them once. Just before serving, spread with a little butter and sprinkle with salt and pepper. Makes 4 servings.

# Beef Curry and Rice

*This is a party dish and the more condiments you serve with it, the more fun it is to eat. Put the condiments listed below in small bowls on the table and let your guests serve themselves.*

4 tablespoons seedless raisins
½ cup sherry
2 tablespoons butter
1 cup peeled apple slices
1 cup chopped onion
2 pounds ground beef
2 tablespoons flour
3 teaspoons curry powder
1½ teaspoons salt
1 teaspoon ground ginger
1 teaspoon sugar
1 tablespoon lemon juice
1 cup chopped peeled tomatoes (fresh or canned)
1¼ cups water
½ cup unsalted peanuts
Cooked rice
Condiments (see next page)

Soak the raisins in the sherry for 15 minutes. Heat the butter in a deep skillet and sauté the apple and onion until the onion is soft. Add the beef and stir until browned. Sprinkle with the flour and curry powder and stir until the flour disappears. Add all the remaining ingredients except the condiments. Stir until the mixture begins to boil. Cover and simmer very gently for 2 hours. Serve on top of generous servings of rice. Makes 6–8 servings.

CONDIMENTS

Serve any or all of the following: chopped candied ginger; chopped scallions (green onion); chutney; peanuts and cashews; sliced banana sprinkled with lemon juice; coconut (preferably unsweetened); chopped green pepper; cubed cucumber; chopped hard-cooked egg.

# SAUCES for GROUND MEAT DISHES

❂❀❂❀❂❀❂❀❂❀❂❀❂❀❂❀❂❀❂❀❂❀❂❀❂❀❂❀❂❀❂❀❂❀

MANY OF THE SAUCES in this chapter have been mentioned in recipes throughout this book. The Creole Sauce for Creole Stuffed Peppers (p. 52) is here, as is the Taco Sauce for Tacos (p. 133). In addition there are sauces here for improvisation, sauces that do not go with any specific recipe. Some are excellent for dressing up leftovers or to serve on basic hamburgers, meat loaf and meatballs. Others are excellent substitutes for other sauces suggested in recipes. For example, try pouring Cumberland Sauce over African-Style Meat Loaf (p. 194) instead of the Tomato Sauce called for in the recipe. Or vary the Meatball Heros with Barbecue Sauce (p. 127) by trying them with a variety of different barbecue sauces.

Certain sauces, like Tomato Sauce (p. 263), are very good to have on hand at all times in the freezer, since they are used so frequently with so many dishes. Store sauces in heavy-duty plastic containers or freezer jars of varying sizes, leaving a one-inch space to allow for expansion during freezing. It's fine to have a large container of spaghetti sauce in the freezer, but it's also good to have half-pint and pint containers for those many times when you will want only a cup or two of sauce.

Most sauces will keep for up to six months in the freezer. When you want to reheat a sauce, place the container in barely simmering water and let thaw until the sauce is loose enough to transfer to a saucepan. Your sauce may separate while reheating, but all you have to do is whip or stir it back together.

When reheating a sauce, check the seasonings, especially the salt, which tends to disappear during freezing. The reverse is true of black pepper, garlic, cloves, green pepper and celery, which increase in strength while frozen, so be careful not to overseason sauces if you plan to freeze them.

# Tomato Sauce

*This meatless tomato sauce is the backbone for many of the dishes in this book. In the late summer, when tomatoes are at their peak and your energies are high, make this sauce in double or even quadruple quantities and freeze it in containers of varying sizes. You'll thank yourself all winter long.*

2 tablespoons butter
2 tablespoons olive oil
½ cup grated onion
2 cloves garlic, minced
5 cups peeled, seeded and chopped tomatoes or
   1 large can (35 ounces) Italian plum tomatoes
1 can tomato paste
2 cups water
½ cup red wine
½ teaspoon sugar
¾ teaspoon salt
¼ teaspoon pepper
¼ teaspoon thyme
¼ teaspoon basil
4 sprigs of parsley
1 bay leaf
⅛ teaspoon oregano

Heat the butter and the oil in a deep, heavy pan. Sauté the onion and garlic until just tender. Add the remaining ingredients. Bring the sauce to a boil and simmer partially covered for 1 hour, or longer if a very thick sauce is desired. Remove the bay leaf and parsley. Makes about 5 cups.

## Ten-Minute Tomato Sauce

*There are occasions when you simply do not have enough time to prepare a long-simmering sauce, but you need tomato sauce all the same. This one takes only ten minutes to prepare, and any leftovers can be frozen.*

2 tablespoons butter
2 tablespoons olive oil
½ cup chopped onion
1 large clove garlic, minced
1 can (35 ounces) Italian plum tomatoes or tomato puree
1 tablespoon chopped parsley
½ teaspoon oregano
2 tablespoons tomato paste
¼ teaspoon sugar
2 teaspoons salt
¼ teaspoon pepper

Heat the butter and oil in a saucepan. Add the onion and garlic and cook gently until tender. Add the remaining ingredients and cook for 8 minutes, stirring frequently. Spin very briefly in the blender. Makes about 4 cups.

# Tomato-Meat Sauce

*This very basic tomato and meat sauce should be a staple in your freezer.*

1 onion, chopped
1 clove garlic, minced
2 tablespoons oil or butter
¾ pound ground beef
1 can (16 ounces) Italian plum tomatoes
1 can (6 ounces) tomato paste
1 teaspoon salt
½ teaspoon sugar
¼ teaspoon basil
¼ teaspoon thyme
Few sprigs of parsley
1 bay leaf
1 cup red wine
2 cups water

In a heavy 6-quart kettle sauté the onion and garlic in oil until lightly browned. Add the meat and brown for 2–3 minutes, stirring with a fork; pour off excess fat. Add the remaining ingredients. Stir well and simmer for 2 hours, stirring occasionally. Remove the bay leaf. Makes about 4 servings.

## Meat-Mushroom Sauce

1 pound Italian sausage meat
2 pounds ground beef
4 large onions, chopped
6 cloves garlic, minced
1 cup chopped parsley
¾ pound mushrooms, sliced
6 cups Tomato Sauce (p. 263)
1 fifth (4/5 quart) dry red table wine
1½ teaspoons salt
1 teaspoon sage
1 teaspoon rosemary
½ teaspoon marjoram
½ teaspoon thyme
½ teaspoon basil
Pepper

In a large kettle or Dutch oven slowly brown the sausage meat. Add the ground beef and brown, stirring to break it up. Drain off excess fat. Add the onions and garlic and sauté until the onions are limp. Stir in the parsley and mushrooms and then add the remaining ingredients. Cover loosely and simmer for about 3 hours, stirring occasionally, until it is reduced to a thick sauce. Skim off any excess fat. Makes about 3 quarts.

## Creole Sauce

2 tablespoons butter
1 onion, chopped
½ cup diced celery
3 cups Tomato Sauce (p. 263)
1 cup water
1 bay leaf
2 whole cloves
Salt and pepper

Heat the butter in a skillet and sauté the onion and celery
for 5 minutes. Add the Tomato Sauce, water, bay leaf,
cloves and salt and pepper to taste. Simmer for 15 minutes.
Makes about 3½ cups.

## Taco Sauce

*If the stores in your area don't stock taco sauce, try making
your own. This is not bona fide Mexican, but it's a close
and easy-to-make approximation.*

1 cup Tomato Sauce (p. 263)
2 tablespoons vinegar
1 tablespoon oil
2 cloves garlic, crushed
¼ teaspoon oregano, crumbled
1 jar (4 ounces) green chilies, drained and chopped fine
½–¾ teaspoon hot pepper sauce

Combine all the ingredients in the order given and mix
well. Makes about 1½ cups.

## Tomato Barbecue Sauce

*You can serve this or any of the following barbecue sauces with any number of meat loaves, including the Basic Meat Loaf (p. 177) and Speedy Meat Loaf (p. 178). Or try a sauce on Sausage-Stuffed Meat Loaf (p. 184), Piquant Meat Loaf (p. 187), or Rice Meat Loaf (p. 191), to name a few. Pour the sauce over the loaves after baking or brush it on 15 minutes before the loaves are done. Serve a barbecue sauce over hamburgers, too, or substitute one of these recipes for the barbecue sauces given in Barbecued Beef on Rolls (p. 129) or Meatball Heroes with Barbecue Sauce (p. 127).*

1 teaspoon seasoned salt
½ teaspoon seasoned pepper
1 tablespoon paprika
1 tablespoon sugar
½ teaspoon garlic salt
1 teaspoon minced onion
1 cup catsup
½ cup water
⅓ cup vinegar
1 tablespoon steak sauce
2 tablespoons butter

Mix all the dry ingredients together. Add the catsup, water and vinegar and put in a saucepan; bring to a boil. Remove from the heat and stir in the steak sauce and butter. Makes about 2 cups.

# Herb Barbecue Sauce

1 cup catsup
½ cup water
3 tablespoons tarragon vinegar
¼ teaspoon oregano
¼ teaspoon marjoram
¼ teaspoon thyme
¼ teaspoon garlic salt
1 tablespoon steak sauce

Combine all the ingredients together. Makes about 1¾ cups.

# Barbados Barbecue Sauce

½ cup molasses
⅓ cup prepared mustard
½ cup vinegar
2 tablespoons Worcestershire sauce
½ teaspoon hot pepper sauce
1 cup catsup

Combine all the ingredients together and mix well. Makes about 2⅓ cups.

# Deep South Hot Barbecue Sauce

*Especially good on Piquant Meat Loaf (p. 187).*

1 onion, chopped
1 clove garlic, minced
2 tablespoons oil
1 can (10½ ounces) tomato puree
1 cup chili sauce
1 cup vinegar
1 bottle (7 ounces) ginger ale
1 teaspoon cracked black pepper
2 teaspoons seasoned pepper
1 tablespoon salt
¼ cup sugar
1 tablespoon ground allspice
1 teaspoon mace
¼ teaspoon hot pepper sauce

Cook the onion and garlic in the oil for 10 minutes, stirring often. Add the remaining ingredients and simmer for about 15 minutes. Makes about 3 cups.

# Curry Barbecue Sauce

2 tablespoons curry powder
1½ teaspoons garlic salt
1 tablespoon dry mustard
2 tablespoons steak sauce
½ cup butter, melted
⅔ cup red wine vinegar

Combine all the ingredients and blend until smooth. Makes about 1¼ cups.

# Brown Gravy I

Whether ground meat has been panfried or baked, there will be drippings that will lend themselves to brown gravy. For every cup of gravy desired, measure 2 tablespoons of drippings, adding butter or margarine if necessary. Heat until the fat bubbles, scraping the bottom of the pan. Stir in 2 tablespoons flour and stir for a few minutes until browned. Add 1 cup beef stock or bouillon or a cup of boiling water fortified with a beef bouillon cube. Stir with a whisk until smooth. Season with salt, pepper and a pinch of dried herbs (parsley, thyme, bay leaf). Makes about 1 cup.

# Brown Gravy II

If you need gravy but have no pan drippings, brown ½ cup grated onion and ¼ cup grated carrot in 3 tablespoons butter or margarine. (Be careful not to let the vegetables burn.) Add 2 tablespoons flour and stir for a few minutes until lightly browned. Add 1 cup beef stock, canned bouillon or boiling water fortified with a bouillon cube. Stir until smooth, then add a few drops of gravy coloring. Season well with salt and pepper. Strain before serving. Makes about 1 cup.

## Chili Sauce Topping

*Serve with Texas Bean Bake (p. 80) or Hamburger and Hot Dog Casserole (p. 89). It's terrific over hamburgers and meat loaves, too.*

½ cup chili sauce
⅓ cup packed brown sugar
2 tablespoons lemon juice
1 teaspoon dry mustard
Freshly ground black pepper

Blend all the ingredients together, adding pepper to taste. Makes about ¾ cup.

## Marinara Sauce

*This is a handy sauce for any number of meat loaves, including African-Style Meat Loaf (p. 194) and Hamburger and Egg Meat Loaf (p. 183), as well as for many main dishes such as Grecian Hamburgers (p. 34) and Beef Patties Parmigiana (p. 37).*

¼ cup finely chopped onion
2 cloves garlic, minced
¼ cup olive oil
1 can (35 ounces) Italian plum tomatoes
1 can (6 ounces) tomato paste
1 cup water
¼ cup chopped parsley
1 teaspoon basil
½ teaspoon each salt and sugar
⅛ teaspoon crushed red pepper
Dash of pepper

In a saucepan cook the onion and garlic in the oil until tender. Add the remaining ingredients and bring to a boil, then simmer, uncovered, for about 1 hour, or until the sauce is of the desired consistency. Makes about 3 cups.

## Brown Mushroom Sauce

*Serve with Meat-Filled Manicotti (p. 236) or with other hamburgers and meat loaves.*

1 tablespoon chopped shallots or scallions (green onion)
¼ pound mushrooms, sliced thin
3 tablespoons butter
1 teaspoon lemon juice
1 cup leftover or commercially prepared beef gravy

Cook the shallots or scallion and mushrooms in the butter, stirring occasionally, for 5 minutes. Add the remaining ingredients and heat. Makes about 2 cups.

## Golden Mushroom Sauce

*Perfect for serving over many hamburgers and meat loaves.*

¼ pound mushrooms, sliced
2 tablespoons butter
2 tablespoons flour
1 cup chicken bouillon
1 teaspoon lemon juice
Salt and pepper
Slivered almonds (optional)

Sauté the mushrooms in the butter for 2–3 minutes. Sprinkle with flour and mix well. Add the bouillon and cook, stirring, until thickened. Stir in the lemon juice and salt and pepper to taste. Add a few almonds if desired. Makes about 1¼ cups.

## Creamy Horseradish Sauce

*For meat loaf; try it with Specialty Meat Loaf (p. 186) or Blue-Cheese Meat Loaf (p. 199).*

1 cup heavy cream
½ teaspoon salt
3–4 tablespoons prepared horseradish

Whip the cream until it is stiff. Add the salt and horse-radish. Makes about 2 cups.

# Creamy Mustard Sauce

1 cup light cream
¼ cup sugar
2 tablespoons dry mustard
1 tablespoon flour
¼ teaspoon salt
1 egg yolk, beaten

Scald ¾ cup of the cream in the top part of a small double boiler over boiling water. Add the sugar. Mix the mustard, flour and salt together and then add the remaining cream to make a smooth mixture. Stir this into the cream in the double boiler and cook, stirring, until thickened. Stir a little of the cream mixture into the egg yolk, then add the egg yolk to the double boiler and cook, stirring, for 2 minutes. Remove from the heat and stir in ½ cup hot water. Makes about 1⅓ cups.

# Sweet-Sour Sauce

1 tablespoon cornstarch
¼ cup sugar
1 tablespoon prepared mustard
1½ tablespoons meat loaf drippings or butter
¼ cup vinegar

In a small saucepan mix the cornstarch and sugar. Add 1 cup water and cook, stirring, until thickened. Add the remaining ingredients and mix until blended. Heat well and serve on sliced meat loaf. Makes about 1¼ cups.

## Cumberland Sauce

*Serve this luscious sauce over hamburgers, meatballs, Basic Meat Loaf (p. 177), or try it over African-Style Meat Loaf (p. 194) to intensify the loaf's fruity flavor.*

1 cup port wine
½ cup golden raisins
½ cup red currant jelly
1 teaspoon dry mustard
¼ teaspoon ground ginger
1 teaspoon grated lemon peel
2 tablespoons cornstarch blended with ¼ cup orange juice

In a saucepan over medium heat bring to a boil the port, raisins, jelly, mustard, ginger and lemon peel. Gradually stir the blended cornstarch into the hot mixture and cook, stirring, until thickened. Makes about 1¾ cups.

## Dill and Sour Cream Sauce

*Wonderful with Individual Stroganoff Meat Loaves (p. 193) or over hot meatballs.*

2 tablespoons flour
1 tablespoon snipped fresh dillweed
½ teaspoon sugar
1 cup sour cream
1 cup pan juices or beef broth

Vigorously stir the flour, dillweed, sugar and sour cream into the pan juices. Cook, stirring, until bubbly. Makes about 1¾ cups.

# Herb Butter Sauce

*For any basic meat loaf.*

2 tablespoons butter
¼ teaspoon powdered thyme
¼ teaspoon sage
1 tablespoon chopped parsley

Mix the ingredients together well. Spread on a hot loaf just before serving. Makes enough for one 9-by-5-by-3-inch loaf.

# Cheese Sauce

2 tablespoons butter
2 tablespoons flour
1½ cups milk
1 cup grated medium-sharp Cheddar cheese
½ teaspoon salt
⅛ teaspoon white pepper
Dash of cayenne
⅛ teaspoon nutmeg
1 teaspoon prepared mustard (optional)

Heat the butter in a small saucepan and stir in the flour. Cook over medium heat for 2 minutes without browning. Add the milk and whisk until smooth and thick. Add the remaining ingredients and stir until the cheese melts. Makes about 2 cups.

# INDEX